ExpressWays

ENGLISH FOR COMMUNICATION

1A

Steven J. Molinsky · Bill Bliss

 PRENTICE HALL REGENTS, Englewood Cliffs, New Jersey 07632

Library of Congress Cataloging-in-Publication Data
(Revised for vol. 1)

Molinsky, Steven J.
  ExpressWays : English for communication.

  Includes indexes.
  1. English language—Text-books for foreign speakers.
I. Bliss, Bill. II. Title.
PE1128.M674 1986   428.3'4   85-30059
ISBN 0-13-298423-7 (v. 1)

Editorial/production supervision and
   interior design: Sylvia Moore
Development: Ellen Lehrburger
Cover design: Lundgren Graphics, Ltd.
Manufacturing buyer: Lorraine Fumoso
Page layout: Diane Koromhas

Illustrations and cover drawing by Gabriel Polonsky

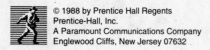

© 1988 by Prentice Hall Regents
Prentice-Hall, Inc.
A Paramount Communications Company
Englewood Cliffs, New Jersey 07632

Printed in the United States of America

20 19 18 17 16 15 14 13 12

ISBN 0-13-298431-8

Prentice-Hall International (UK) Limited, *London*
Prentice-Hall of Australia Pty. Limited, *Sydney*
Prentice-Hall Canada Inc., *Toronto*
Prentice-Hall Hispanoamericana, S.A., *Mexico*
Prentice-Hall of India Private Limited, *New Delhi*
Prentice-Hall of Japan, Inc., *Tokyo*
Prentice-Hall of Southeast Asia Pte. Ltd., *Singapore*
Editora Prentice-Hall do Brasil, Ltda., *Rio de Janeiro*

Contents

Singular/Plural • Prepositions of Location • Adjectives
• Too + Adjective • Ordinal Numbers • Want to
• Question Formation

Want-Desire • Directions-Location • Satisfaction/Dissatisfaction
• Attracting Attention • Gratitude
• Checking and Indicating Understanding • Hesitating

CHAPTER EIGHT

EMPLOYMENT/ON THE JOB

Past Tense • Imperatives • Object Pronouns
• Time Expressions • Can • Could • Adjectives
• Prepositions of Location • Singular/Plural

Requests • Instructing • Attracting Attention • Approval/Disapproval
• Apologizing • Checking and Indicating Understanding
• Asking for Repetition • Hesitating • Focusing Attention

CHAPTER NINE

RECREATION • SOCIAL COMMUNICATION
• EMPLOYMENT/ON THE JOB • WEATHER

Past Tense • WH-Questions • Future: Going to • Want to
• Like to • Like to vs. Like • Can • Have to
• Time Expressions

Want-Desire • Asking for and Reporting Information • Invitations
• Likes/Dislikes • Intention • Obligation
• Checking and Indicating Understanding

SCENES & IMPROVISATIONS:
CHAPTERS 7, 8, 9

APPENDIX

CHAPTER-BY-CHAPTER SUMMARY OF FUNCTIONS
AND CONVERSATION STRATEGIES
TOPIC VOCABULARY GLOSSARY
IRREGULAR VERBS

INDEXES

INDEX OF FUNCTIONS AND CONVERSATION
STRATEGIES
INDEX OF TOPICS
INDEX OF GRAMMATICAL STRUCTURES

TO THE TEACHER

ExpressWays is a functional English program for adult and young-adult learners of English. The program consists of the following components:

Student Course Books—offering intensive conversational practice;

Companion Workbooks—offering grammar, reading, writing, and listening comprehension practice fully coordinated with the student course books;

Guide Books—providing background notes and expansion activities for all lessons and step-by-step instructions for teachers;

Audio Program—offering realistic presentation of dialogs in the texts;

Picture Program—including Picture Cards for vocabulary development and Dialog Visual Cards that depict scenes and characters from the texts;

Placement and Achievement Testing Program—providing tools for the evaluation of student levels and progress.

ExpressWays—Book 1 is intended for adult and young-adult students of English at the beginning level. The text provides an introduction to basic grammar and vocabulary and the usage of English for everyday life situations. *ExpressWays—Book 1* is organized by topics, or competencies, while incorporating integrated coverage of functions and beginning-level grammar.*

THE DIMENSIONS OF COMMUNICATION: FUNCTION, FORM, AND CONTENT

A number of texts present a "topical," or competency-based, syllabus by covering vocabulary items and key expressions needed for specific situations. A number of other texts present a "functional" syllabus by describing language use and listing sets of functional phrases. In both cases, texts tend to focus exclusively on the one dimension of communication that organizes the syllabus. In addition, both topical and functional texts do not usually give students intensive communicative practice using the correct grammatical forms that are required by particular key expressions or functional language choices.

---

* *ExpressWays—Books 1 and 2* are organized by a spiralled curriculum. They are based on a core topical curriculum that is covered at different degrees of intensity and depth at each level. *ExpressWays—Book 1* provides students with the most important vocabulary, grammar, and functional expressions needed to communicate at a basic level in a full range of situations and contexts. *ExpressWays—Book 2* covers the same full range of situations and contexts, but offers students expanded vocabulary, more complex grammar, and a wider choice of functional expressions.

ExpressWays—Book 3 is organized by functions, while incorporating integrated coverage of higher level topics and grammar. *ExpressWays—Foundations* is a simplified edition of Book 1, for students who require more basic material and who perhaps have more limited reading and writing skills.

ExpressWays—Book 1 aims to provide dynamic, communicative practice that involves students in lively interactions based on the content of real-life contexts and situations. The topically organized syllabus is fully integrated into a complete conversational course in which students not only learn the vocabulary and expressions needed for essential life situations, but also learn the various ways to express the functions of English and intensively practice the grammatical forms required to competently produce these expressions and functions.

Every lesson in the program offers students simultaneous practice with one or more functions, the grammatical forms needed to express those functions, and the contexts and situations in which the functions and grammar are used. This "tri-dimensional clustering" of function, form, and content is the organizing principle behind each lesson and the cornerstone of the *ExpressWays* approach to functional syllabus design.

ExpressWays aims to offer students broad exposure to uses of language in a variety of relevant contexts: in community, academic, employment, home, and social settings. The characters portrayed are people of different ages, ethnic groups, and occupations, interacting in real-life situations.

While some texts make a point of giving students a range of ways of expressing a function, from extremely polite to very impolite, we have chosen to "take the middle ground" and concentrate on those expressions that would most frequently occur in normal polite conversation between people in various settings. *ExpressWays* does offer a variety of registers, from the formal language someone might use in a job interview, with a customer, or when speaking with an authority figure, to the informal language someone would use when talking with family members, co-workers, or friends.

A special feature of the program is the treatment of discourse strategies. Students actively practice initiating conversations and topics, hesitating, checking and indicating understanding, and other conversation skills.

AN OVERVIEW

Guided Conversations

Guided Conversations are the dialogs and exercises that are the central learning devices in the program. Each lesson begins with a model guided conversation that depicts a real-life situation and the vocabulary, grammar, and functions used in the communication exchange. In the exercises that follow, students create new conversations by placing new contexts, content, or characters into the framework of the model.

"Now Present Your Own Conversations"

Each lesson ends with this open-ended exercise which offers students the opportunity to create and present original conversations based on the model. Students contribute content based on their experiences, ideas, and imaginations, while staying within the framework of the model.

We should emphasize that the objective of each lesson is to provide a measure of controlled practice with a dialog and guided conversation exercises so that students can competently create their own, original conversations.

Interchange

This end-of-chapter activity offers students the opportunity to create and present "guided role plays." Each activity consists of a model that students can practice and then use as a basis for their original presentations. Students should be encouraged to be inventive and to use new vocabulary in these presentations and should feel free to adapt and expand the model any way they wish.

Scenes & Improvisations

These "free role plays" appear after every third chapter, offering review and synthesis of lessons in the three preceding chapters. Students are presented with eight scenes depicting conversations between people in various situations. They use the information in the scenes to determine who the people are and what they are talking about. Then, students improvise based on their perceptions of the scenes' characters, contexts, and situations.

The purpose of these improvisations is to offer free recombination practice that promotes students' absorption of the preceding chapters' vocabulary, grammar, and functions into their repertoire of active language use.

Support and Reference Sections

ExpressWays offers a number of support and reference sections:

- *Chapter Opening Pages* provide an overview of topics, grammar, and key functions and conversation strategies highlighted in each chapter.
- *End-of-Chapter Summaries* provide complete lists of topic vocabulary and grammar structures appearing in each chapter.
- A *Chapter-by-Chapter Summary of Functions and Conversation Strategies* in the Appendix provides an overview of all expressions for the functions and conversation strategies in each chapter.
- A *Topic Vocabulary Glossary* provides a listing of key vocabulary domains included in the text and indicates the pages where the words first appear.
- An *Index of Functions and Conversation Strategies*, an *Index of Topics* and an *Index of Grammatical Structures* provide a convenient reference for locating coverage of functions, topics, and grammar in the text.

THE TOTAL *ExpressWays* PROGRAM

The *ExpressWays Student Course Books* are essentially designed to offer intensive communicative practice. These texts may be used independently, or in conjunction with the *ExpressWays Companion Workbooks*, which offer practice in the other skill areas of reading, writing, and listening, as well as focused practice with particular grammar structures as they occur in the program. Each exercise in the Companion Workbook indicates the specific Student Course Book page that it corresponds to.

The *ExpressWays Guide Books* provide step-by-step instructions for coverage of each lesson, background notes, sample answers to guided conversation exercises, and answer keys and listening-activity scripts for exercises in the Companion Workbooks. For teachers of multi-level classes, the Guide Books indicate for each lesson the corresponding page in *ExpressWays—Foundations* that covers the same topic at a lower level, and the corresponding page in *ExpressWays—Book 2* that covers the same topic at a higher level.

Perhaps the most important feature of the Guide Books is the expansion exercise that is recommended for each lesson. These exercises offer students free, spontaneous practice with the vocabulary, grammar, and functions that are presented in the Student Course Books. Activities include improvisations, "information gap" role plays, problem-solving, and topics for discussion and debate. We encourage teachers to use these activities or similar ones as springboards to help their students "break away" from the text and incorporate lesson content into their everyday use of English.

The *ExpressWays Audio Program* includes a set of tapes providing realistic presentation of all model dialogs and selected guided conversation exercises in the Student Course Books. The tapes are designed to be used interactively, so that the recorded voice serves as the student's speaking partner, making conversation practice possible even when the student is studying alone. The Audio Program also includes a set of tapes for the listening comprehension exercises in the Companion Workbooks.

The *ExpressWays Picture Program* includes Dialog Visual Cards and Picture Cards. The *ExpressWays Dialog Visual Cards* are poster-size illustrations depicting the characters and settings of all model dialogs. Their use during introduction of the model helps to assure that students are engaged in active listening and speaking practice during this important stage in the lesson. The *ExpressWays Picture Cards* illustrate key concepts and vocabulary items. They can be used for introduction of new material, for review, for enrichment exercises, and for role-playing activities.

The *ExpressWays Testing Program* includes a Placement Testing Kit for initial evaluation and leveling of students, and sets of Mid-Term and Final Examinations to measure students' achievement at each level of the program. All tests in the program include both oral and written evaluation components.

SUGGESTED TEACHING STRATEGIES

In using *ExpressWays,* we encourage you to develop approaches and strategies that are compatible with your own teaching style and the needs and abilities of your students. While the program does not require any specific method or technique in order to be used effectively, you may find it helpful to review and try out some of the following suggestions. (Specific step-by-step instructions may be found in the Guide Books.)

Guided Conversations

1. *Setting the Scene.* Have students look at the model illustration in the book or on the *ExpressWays* Dialog Visual Card. Set the scene: Who are the people? What is the situation?
2. *Listening to the Model.* With books closed, have students listen to the model conversation—presented by you, a pair of students, or on the audio tape.
3. *Class Practice.* With books still closed, model each line and have the whole class repeat in unison.
4. *Reading.* With books open, have students follow along as two students present the model.

   (At this point, ask students if they have any questions and check understanding of new vocabulary. You may also want to call students' attention to any related language or culture notes, which can be found in the Guide Book.)
5. *Pair Practice.* In pairs, have students practice the model conversation.
6. *Exercise Practice.* (optional) Have pairs of students simultaneously practice all the exercises.
7. *Exercise Presentations.* Call on pairs of students to present the exercises.

   (At this point, you may want to discuss any language or culture notes related to the exercises, as indicated in the Guide Book.)

"Now Present Your Own Conversations"

In these activities that follow the guided conversations at the end of each lesson, have pairs of students create and present original conversations based on the model. Encourage students to be inventive as they create their characters and situations. (You may want to assign this exercise as homework, having students prepare their original conversations, practice them the next day with another student, and then present them to the class.) In this way, students can review the previous day's lesson without actually having to repeat the specific exercises already covered.

Expansion

We encourage you to use the expansion activity for each lesson suggested in the Guide Book or a similar activity that provides students with free, spontaneous practice while synthesizing the content of the lesson.

Interchange

Have students practice the model using the same steps listed above for guided conversations. (You might want to eliminate the *Class Practice* step in the case of longer Interchange dialogs.) After practicing the model, have pairs of students create and present original conversations using the model dialog as a guide. Encourage students to be inventive and to use new vocabulary. (You may want to assign this exercise as homework, having students prepare their own conversations, practice them the next day with another student, and then present them to the class.) Students should present their conversations without referring to the written text, but they should also not memorize them. Rather, they should feel free to adapt and expand them any way they wish.

Scenes & Improvisations

Have students talk about the people and the situations, and then present role plays based on the scenes. Students may refer back to previous lessons as a resource, but they should not simply re-use specific conversations. (You may want to assign these exercises as written homework, having students prepare their conversations, practice them the next day with another student, and then present them to the class.)

Multi-Level Classes

Teachers of multi-level classes may wish to modify some of the teaching suggestions mentioned above. For example, teachers who have their students do simultaneous pair practice can have students at lower levels practice fewer exercises while students at higher levels practice more or all exercises. During this pair practice, the teacher can offer special help to students at lower levels and perhaps tell them which particular exercise they should prepare for presentation to the class.

For multi-level classes with an exceptionally wide range of ability levels, the *Express-Ways—Book 1 Guide Books* indicate for each lesson the corresponding page in *Express-Ways—Foundations* that covers the same topic at a lower level and the corresponding page in *ExpressWays—Book 2* that covers the same topic at a higher level.

In conclusion, we have attempted to offer students a communicative, meaningful, and lively way of practicing the vocabulary, grammar, and functions of English. While conveying to you the substance of our textbook, we hope that we have also conveyed the spirit: that learning to communicate in English can be genuinely interactive . . . truly relevant to our students' lives . . . and fun!

Steven J. Molinsky
Bill Bliss

Components of an ExpressWays Lesson

A **model conversation** offers initial practice with the functions and structures of the lesson.

In the **exercises**, students create conversations by placing new contexts, content, or characters into the model.

The **open-ended exercise** at the end of each lesson asks students to create and present original conversations based on the model.

Examples:

Exercise 1:

A. Excuse me. Does this train go to Brooklyn?
B. No, it doesn't. It goes to the Bronx.
A. Oh, I see. Tell me, which train goes to Brooklyn?
B. The "D" Train.
A. Thanks very much.

Exercise 2:

A. Excuse me. Does this plane go to San Francisco?
B. No, it doesn't. It goes to San Diego.
A. Oh, I see. Tell me, which plane goes to San Francisco?
B. Flight 64.
A. Thanks very much.

- **PERSONAL INFORMATION**
- **SOCIAL COMMUNICATION**

- To Be • To Be: Yes/No Questions
  • WH-Questions

Hello
I'd Like to Introduce . . .
What's Your Last Name?
What's Your Address?
Where Are You From?
Nice to Meet You

• Greeting People • Introductions
• Asking for and Reporting Information

Hello

Carlos   Kim

A. Hello. My name is Carlos.

B. Hi. I'm Kim. Nice to meet you.

A. Nice meeting you, too.

Doris   Jane

1.

Tom   Karen

2.

Mary   Bob
Warner   Wilson

3.

Richard   Steve
Simon   Smith

4.

Brian   Jessica

5.

Now present your own
conversations.

I'd Like to Introduce . . .

my husband, Michael

A. Hi! How are you?

B. Fine. And you?

A. Fine, thanks. I'd like to introduce you to my husband, Michael.

B. Nice to meet you.

1. my wife, Barbara

2. my father, Mr. Peterson

3. my mother, Mrs. Chen

4. my brother, George

5. my sister, Irene

Now present your own conversations.

What's Your Last Name?

Maria Sanchez

A. What's your last name?

B. Sanchez.

A. Could you spell that, please?

B. S-A-N-C-H-E-Z.

A. And your first name?

B. Maria.

1. John Clayton

2. Nancy Brenner

3. Linda Kwan

4. Robert Kelton

5. Lefty Grimes

Now present your own conversations.

What's Your Address?

10 Main Street
423-6978

A. What's your address?

B. 10 Main Street.

A. And your telephone number?

B. 423-6978.

1. 5 Summer Street
531-7624

2. 7 Pond Road
899-3263

3. 14 Maple Avenue
475-1182

4. 19 Howard Road
542-7306*

5. 1813† Central Avenue
733-8920

Now present your own
conversations.

* 0 = "oh"
† 1813 = eighteen thirteen

5

Where Are You From?

A. What's your name?

B. Kenji.

A. Where are you from?

B. Japan.

A. Oh. Are you from Tokyo?

B. No. I'm from Osaka.

1. Maria
Italy

2. Hector
Mexico

3. Mohammed
Egypt

4. Anna
The Soviet Union

5. Mei Ling
China

Now present your own
conversations.

INTERCHANGE
Nice to Meet You

A. Hello. My name is Franco Rossi.

B. Hello. I'm Harry Miller.

A. Are you American?

B. Yes, I am. I'm from New York.
de How about you? *donde es ustd*

A. I'm Italian. I'm from Rome.

B. Nice to meet you.

A. Nice meeting you, too.

Franco Rossi	Harry Miller
Italian	American
Rome	New York

1. Carol Williams   Carmen Lopez
Canadian   Mexican
Toronto   Mexico City

2. Charles Whitmore   Ali Hassan
British   Egyptian
London   Cairo

3. David Clarke   Asako Tanaka
Australian   Japanese
Melbourne   Tokyo

4. Rick Starlight   Natasha Markova
American   Russian
Hollywood   Moscow

You're an airplane passenger on an international flight. Create an original conversation using the model dialog above as a guide. Feel free to adapt and expand the model any way you wish.

CHAPTER 1 SUMMARY

Topic Vocabulary

Personal Information

- name
- last name
- first name
- address
- street
- road
- avenue
- telephone number

Family Members

- husband
- wife
- father
- mother
- brother
- sister

Countries

- China
- Egypt
- Italy
- Japan
- Mexico
- The Soviet Union

Nationalities

- American
- Australian
- British
- Canadian
- Egyptian
- Italian
- Japanese
- Mexican
- Russian

Grammar

To Be

My name **is** Carlos.
I'm Kim.
I'm from Osaka.
I'm Italian.

To Be: Yes/No Questions

Are you from Tokyo?
Yes, I **am**.

WH-Questions

What's your name?
Where are you from?

Cardinal Numbers: 1–19

1	one	11	eleven
2	two	12	twelve
3	three	13	thirteen
4	four	14	fourteen
5	five	15	fifteen
6	six	16	sixteen
7	seven	17	seventeen
8	eight	18	eighteen
9	nine	19	nineteen
10	ten		

Functions and Conversation Strategies in this chapter are listed in the Appendix, **page A-1**.

2

- **TELEPHONE** • **GETTING AROUND TOWN**
  • **SOCIAL COMMUNICATION**

- **Subject Pronouns** • **To Be: Am/Is/Are**
  • **To Be: Yes/No Questions**
  • **To Be: Negative Sentences**
- **Present Continuous Tense** • **Possessive Adjectives**
  • **WH-Questions**

I'd Like the Number of Mary Nielson
I'm Sorry. You Have the Wrong Number
Is Peter There?
Where Are You Going?
What Are You Doing?
I Can't Talk Right Now. I'm Taking a Shower

• Asking for and Reporting Information • Greeting People
• Identifying • Leave Taking

I'd Like the Number of Mary Nielson

A. Directory assistance. What city?

B. Chicago. I'd like the number of Mary Nielson.

A. How do you spell that?

B. N-I-E-L-S-O-N.

A. What street?

B. Hudson Avenue.

A. Just a moment . . . The number is 863-4227.

1. 968-3135

2. 747-6360

3. 237-8044

4. 328-1191

5. 623-7575

Now present your own conversations.

I'm Sorry. You Have the Wrong Number

A. Hello.

B. Hello, Fred?

A. I'm sorry.   You have the wrong number.

B. Is this 328-7178?

A. No, it isn't.

B. Oh.   Sorry.

1.

2.

3.

4.

5.

Now present your own
conversations.

Is Peter There?

the supermarket

Peter?

Mike

the bank

Janet?

Patty

the library

Timmy and Billy?

Bobby

A. Hello. This is Mike. Is Peter there?

B. No, he isn't. He's at the supermarket.

A. Oh, I see. I'll call back later. Thank you.

A. Hello. This is Patty. Is Janet there?

B. No, she isn't. She's at the bank.

A. Oh, I see. I'll call back later. Thank you.

A. Hello. This is Bobby. Are Timmy and Billy there?

B. No, they aren't. They're at the library.

A. Oh, I see. I'll call back later. Thank you.

the post office

Fred?

Judy

1.

the laundromat

Susan?

Tim

2.

the clinic

your parents?

Mrs. Gold

3.

the park

Nancy?

Alice

4.

school

Hector?

George

5.

"IS PETER THERE?"

Now present your own conversations.

Where Are You Going?

the post office

the library

A. Hi! How are you today?

B. Fine. And you?

A. Fine, thanks. Where are you going?

B. To the library. How about you?

A. I'm going to the post office.

B. Well, nice seeing you.

A. Nice seeing you, too.

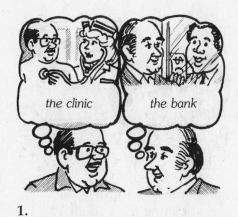

the clinic | the bank

1.

school | the supermarket

2.

the museum | the park

3.

the mall | the movies

4.

the airport | the zoo

5.

"WHERE ARE YOU GOING?"

Now present your own conversations.

What Are You Doing?

A. What are you doing?

B. I'm fixing my car.

A. What's Linda doing?

B. She's studying.

A. What's John doing?

B. He's cleaning the garage.

A. What are you doing?

B. We're doing our homework.

1. Richard
fixing his bicycle

2. you
making breakfast

3. Jennifer and Melissa
cleaning their room

4. Kevin
dancing

5. Miss Henderson
looking for her contact lens

Now present your own
conversations.

INTERCHANGE
I Can't Talk Right Now. I'm Taking a Shower

A. Hello, Steve? This is Jackie.

B. Hi. How are you doing?

A. Pretty good. How about you?

B. Okay. Listen, I can't talk right now. I'm taking a shower.

A. Oh, okay. I'll call back later.

B. Speak to you soon.

A. Good-bye.

Jackie

Steve

taking a shower

Jeff *Pamela*

1. studying

Beth *Debbie*

2. eating lunch

Paul *Glen*

3. cooking dinner

Gloria *Kathy*

4. feeding the baby

A friend is calling you on the telephone, but you can't talk right now. Create an original conversation using the model dialog above as a guide. Feel free to adapt and expand the model any way you wish.

CHAPTER 2 SUMMARY

Topic Vocabulary

Community

airport
bank
clinic
laundromat
library
mall
movies (movie theater)
museum
park
post office
school
supermarket
zoo

Everyday Activities

cleaning (my) room
cleaning the garage
cooking dinner
doing (my) homework
eating lunch
feeding the baby
fixing (my) bicycle
fixing (my) car
making breakfast
studying
taking a shower

Telephone

directory assistance
number

Family Members

baby
parents

Grammar

Subject Pronouns

I   **I'm** sorry.
he   **He's** at the supermarket.
she   **She's** at the bank.
it   No, **it** isn't.
we   **We're** doing our
      homework.
you   How are **you** today?
they   **They're** at the library.

To Be: Am/Is/Are

I **am**   **I'm** going to the post
      office.

he **is**   **Is** Peter there?
she **is**   **Is** Janet there?
it **is**   **Is** this 328-7178?

we **are**   **We're** doing our
      homework.
you **are**   Where **are** you going?
they **are**   **Are** Timmy and Billy
      there?

To Be: Yes/No Questions

Is this 328-7178?
Are Timmy and Billy there?

To Be: Negative Sentences

No, he **isn't**.
No, she **isn't**.
No, it **isn't**.
No, they **aren't**.

Present Continuous Tense

What **is** he do**ing**?
What **is** she do**ing**?
What **are** you do**ing**?
What **are** they do**ing**?

I'm fix**ing** my car.
He's clean**ing** the garage.
She's study**ing**.
We're do**ing** our homework.
They're watch**ing** TV.

Possessive Adjectives

my   I'm fixing **my** car.
his   He's fixing **his** bicycle.
her   She's looking for **her**
      contact lens.
our   We're doing **our**
      homework.
your   What's **your** name?
their   They're cleaning **their**
      room.

WH-Questions

What are you doing**?**
Where are you going**?**
How do you spell that?

Functions and Conversation Strategies in this chapter are listed in the Appendix, **page A-1.**

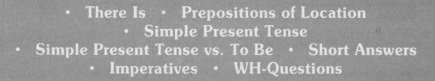

- **GETTING AROUND TOWN**
- **TRANSPORTATION**

3

- There Is • Prepositions of Location
- Simple Present Tense
- Simple Present Tense vs. To Be • Short Answers
- Imperatives • WH-Questions

Is There a Post Office Nearby?
Does This Bus Go to Westville?
Is This Bus Number 42?
Can You Tell Me How to Get to the Bus Station?
Can You Please Tell Me How to Get to the Museum?
Can You Tell Me How to Get to
Franklin's Department Store?
Excuse Me. I'm Lost

- Directions–Location • Asking for and Reporting Information
- Attracting Attention • Gratitude
- Checking and Indicating Understanding • Asking for Repetition

Is There a Post Office Nearby?

A. Excuse me. Is there a post office nearby?

B. Yes. There's a post office on Main Street.

A. On Main Street?

B. Yes. It's on Main Street, next to the bank.

A. Thank you.

A. Excuse me. Is there a laundromat nearby?

B. Yes. There's a laundromat on Grand Avenue.

A. On Grand Avenue?

B. Yes. It's on Grand Avenue, across from the bus station.

A. Thanks.

A. Excuse me. Is there a drug store nearby?

B. Yes. There's a drug store on River Street.

A. On River Street?

B. Yes. It's on River Street, between the library and the clinic.

A. Thanks very much.

A. Excuse me. Is there a supermarket nearby?

B. Yes. There's a supermarket on Davis Boulevard.

A. On Davis Boulevard?

B. Yes. It's on Davis Boulevard, around the corner from the movie theater.

A. Thank you very much.

1. hotel?

2. parking lot?

3. grocery store?

4. gas station?

5. park?

6. clinic?

7. bank?

Now present your own conversations.

Does This Bus Go to Westville?

bus
the Number 30 bus

A. Excuse me. Does this bus go to Westville?

B. No, it doesn't. It goes to Riverside.

A. Oh, I see. Tell me, which bus goes to Westville?

B. The Number 30 bus.

A. Thanks very much.

1. train
   the "D" train

2. plane
   flight 64

3. train
   the "Capitol Express"

4. bus
   Bus Number 27

5. ship
   "The Sunshine Queen"

Now present your own conversations.

Is This Bus Number 42?

A. Is this Bus Number 42?

B. Yes, it is.

A. Oh, good!   I'm on the right bus!

A. Is this the "F" train?

B. No, it isn't.

A. Oops!   I'm on the wrong train!

A. Does this bus stop at Center Street?

B. Yes, it does.

A. Oh, good!   I'm on the right bus!

A. Does this plane go to Florida?

B. No, it doesn't.

A. Oops!   I'm on the wrong plane!

1.

Now present your own conversations.

Can You Tell Me How to Get to the Bus Station?

EMPIRE HOTEL

PARKING LOT

BUS STATION

POST OFFICE

TYLER'S DEPARTMENT STORE

HOSPITAL

LIBRARY

AJAX SUPERMARKET

BANK

on the left

on the right

the bus station?

the post office

A. Excuse me. Can you tell me how to get to the bus station?

B. Yes. Walk THAT way. The bus station is on the left, next to the post office.

A. I'm sorry. Could you please repeat that?

B. All right. Walk THAT way. The bus station is on the left, next to the post office.

A. Thank you.

the library?   the bus station

1.

the Empire Hotel?   the parking lot

2.

the Ajax Supermarket?   the library and the bank

3.

the hospital?   the parking lot

4.

Tyler's Department Store?   the hospital

5.

"CAN YOU TELL ME HOW TO GET TO THE BUS STATION?"

Now present your own conversations.

Can You Please Tell Me How to Get to the Museum?

A. Excuse me. Can you please tell me how to get to the museum?

B. Yes. Walk that way to Second Avenue and turn right.

A. Uh-húh.

B. Then, go two blocks to Grove Street.

A. Okay.

B. Then, turn left on Grove Street and look for the museum on the right. Have you got that?

A. Yes. Thank you very much.

1.

2.

3.

Now present your own conversations.

Can You Tell Me How to Get to Franklin's Department Store?

A. Excuse me. Can you tell me how to get to Franklin's Department Store?

B. Sure. Take the Second Avenue bus and get off at Park Street.

A. I'm sorry. Did you say the Second Avenue bus?

B. Yes. That's right.

A. And WHERE do I get off?

B. At Park Street.

A. Thanks very much.

1.

the Metro Clinic?

the Main Street bus
Central Avenue

2.

the Regency Theater?

the Number 7 train
Broadway

3.

the science museum?

the Red Line
Grove Street

4.

City Hospital?

Bus Number 9
Harrison Road

5.

Riverside Park?

the Parkview bus
Wilson Avenue

"CAN YOU TELL
ME HOW TO GET
TO FRANKLIN'S
DEPARTMENT STORE?"

Now present your own
conversations.

INTERCHANGE
Excuse Me. I'm Lost

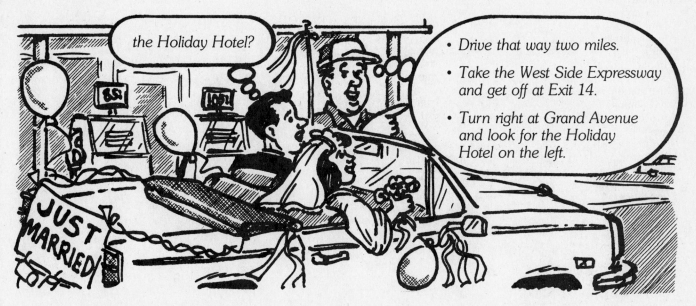

A. Excuse me. I'm lost. Can you possibly tell me how to get to the Holiday Hotel?

B. Sure. Drive that way two miles. Then, take the West Side Expressway and get off at Exit 14. Okay so far?

A. Yes. I'm following you.

B. Then, turn right at Grand Avenue and look for the Holiday Hotel on the left. Have you got that?

A. Yes. I understand. Thanks very much.

A. Excuse me. I'm lost. Can you possibly tell me how to get to _____?

B. Sure. _____.
Then, _____. Okay so far?

A. Yes. I'm following you.

B. Then, _____.
Have you got that?

A. Yes. I understand. Thanks very much.

You're going somewhere by car, by public transportation, or on foot . . . and you're lost! Ask someone for directions. Create an original conversation using the model dialog above as a guide. Feel free to adapt and expand the model any way you wish.

Topic Vocabulary

Community

bank
bus station
clinic
department store
drug store
fire station
gas station
grocery store
hospital
hotel
laundromat
library
movie theater
museum
park
parking lot
police station
post office
shopping mall
supermarket
theater
train station

Transportation

boat
bus
plane
ship
train

expressway
exit

Grammar

There is

Is there a post office nearby?
There's a post office on Main Street.

Prepositions of Location

It's **on** Main Street.
It's **next to** the bank.
It's **across from** the bus station.
It's **between** the library and the clinic.
It's **around the corner from** the movie theater.

Simple Present Tense

Does this bus go to Westville?
No, it **doesn't.**

It **goes** to Riverside.

Simple Present Tense vs. To Be

Is this Bus Number 42?
Yes, it **is.**
No, it **isn't.**

Does this bus stop at Center Street?
Yes, it **does.**
No, it **doesn't.**

Short Answers

Yes, it is.
No, it isn't.

Yes, it does.
No, it doesn't.

Imperatives

Walk that way to Second Avenue.

WH-Questions

Which bus goes to Westville?

Cardinal Numbers: 20–99

20	twenty
21	twenty-one
22	twenty-two
23	twenty-three
•	•
•	•
29	twenty-nine
30	thirty
40	forty
50	fifty
60	sixty
70	seventy
80	eighty
90	ninety
99	ninety-nine

Ordinal Numbers: 1st–5th

1st	first
2nd	second
3rd	third
4th	fourth
5th	fifth

Functions and Conversation Strategies in this chapter are listed in the Appendix, **page A-1.**

SCENES & IMPROVISATIONS
Chapters 1, 2, 3

Who do you think these people are?
What do you think they're talking about?
Create conversations based on these scenes and act them out.

1.

2.

3.

4.

5.

6.

7.

8.

- **HOUSING** · **FOOD**
- **SUPERMARKET**

- **Singular/Plural** · **Count/Non-Count Nouns**
- **This/That/These/Those** · **There Is/There Are**
- **Articles: A/An** · **Article: The** · **Some/Any**
- **Imperatives** · **Have/Has**
- **Simple Present Tense vs. To Be**

We're Looking for a Two-Bedroom
Apartment Downtown
Is There a Refrigerator in the Kitchen?
How Much Is the Rent?
Where Do You Want This Sofa?
There Aren't Any More Cookies
There Isn't Any More Milk
Excuse Me. Where Are the Carrots?
Mmm! This Cake Is Delicious!

- Asking for and Reporting Information · Want–Desire
- Hesitating · Checking and Indicating Understanding

We're Looking for a Two-Bedroom Apartment Downtown

two-bedroom downtown

A. We're looking for a two-bedroom apartment downtown.

B. I think I have an apartment for you.

A. Oh, good. Can you describe it?

B. Yes. It has two bedrooms, a large living room, and a very nice kitchen.

1. three-bedroom near the hospital

2. one-bedroom near the park

3. two-bedroom near the university

4. one-bedroom uptown

5. two-bedroom near the beach

Now present your own conversations.

Is There a Refrigerator in the Kitchen?

a refrigerator – kitchen?

windows – living room?

A. Is there a refrigerator in the kitchen?

B. Yes, there is.   There's a very nice refrigerator in the kitchen.

A. And how many windows are there in the living room?

B. Hmm.   Let me see.   I think there are four windows in the living room.

a shower – bathroom?

cabinets – kitchen?

1.

a fireplace – living room?

closets – bedroom?

2.

a stove – kitchen?

floors – building?

3.

a closet – bedroom?

elevators – building?

4.

a dishwasher – kitchen?

parking spaces – parking lot?

5.

"IS THERE A REFRIGERATOR IN THE KITCHEN?"

Now present your own conversations.

How Much Is the Rent?

A. How much is the rent?

B. It's $700 a month.

A. Does that include utilities?

B. It includes everything except electricity.

A. Hmm. $700 a month plus electricity?

B. That's right.   Do you want to see the apartment?

A. Yes, I think so.

1.

2.

3.

4.

5.

Now present your own conversations.

Where Do You Want This Sofa?

this sofa?

these chairs?

in the living room

in the dining room

A. Where do you want this sofa?

B. That sofa? Hmm. Put it in the living room.

A. And how about these chairs?

B. Those chairs? Let me see. Please put them in the dining room.

this table? in the kitchen

these lamps? in the living room

1.

this bed? in the bedroom

these rugs? near the fireplace

2.

these pictures? next to the sofa

this crib? in the small bedroom

3.

this TV? next to the window

these plants? on the patio

4.

these bicycles? on the balcony

this water bed? in the large bedroom

5.

"WHERE DO YOU WANT THIS SOFA?"

Now present your own conversations.

There Aren't Any More Cookies

a cookie

A. What are you looking for?

B. A cookie.

A. I'm afraid there aren't any more cookies.

B. There aren't?

A. No.   I'll get some more when I go to the supermarket.

a tomato

an apple

a banana

1.

2.

3.

an egg

an orange

"THERE AREN'T ANY MORE COOKIES"

4.

5.

Now present your own conversations.

There Isn't Any More Milk

A. What are you looking for?

B. Milk.

A. I'm afraid there isn't any more milk.

B. There isn't?

A. No. I'll get some more when I go to the supermarket.

1.

2.

3.

4.

5.

Now present your own conversations.

Excuse Me. Where Are the Carrots?

A. Excuse me.   Where are the carrots?

B. They're in Aisle J.

A. I'm sorry.   Did you say "A"?

B. No.   "J."

A. Oh.   Thank you.

A. Excuse me.   Where's the butter?

B. It's in Aisle 3.

A. I'm sorry.   Did you say "C"?

B. No.   "3."

A. Oh.   Thanks.

1.

2.

3.

4.

5.

Now present your own conversations.

INTERCHANGE
Mmm! This Cake Is Delicious!

A. Mmm! This cake is delicious!

B. I'm glad you like it.

A. What's in it?

B. Let me think . . . some eggs, some sugar, some flour, and some raisins.

A. Well, it's excellent!

B. Thank you for saying so.

A. Mmm! These egg rolls are delicious!

B. I'm glad you like them.

A. What's in them?

B. Let me see . . . some cabbage, some pork, some shrimp, and some bean sprouts.

A. Well, they're excellent!

B. Thank you for saying so.

You're eating at your friend's home. The food is delicious. Compliment your friend, using the model dialogs above as a guide. Feel free to adapt and expand the models any way you wish.

Topic Vocabulary

Housing

balcony
bathroom
bedroom
dining room
kitchen
living room
patio

cabinet
closet
dishwasher
fireplace
refrigerator
shower
stove
window

apartment
building

elevator
floor
parking lot
parking space

electricity
gas
heat
parking fee
rent
utilities

Furniture

bed
chair
crib
lamp
picture
plant
rug

sofa
table
TV
waterbed

Foods

apple
banana
bean sprouts
bread
butter
cabbage
cake
carrot
cheese
coffee
cookie
egg
egg rolls
flour

ice cream
lettuce
milk
orange
peach
pork
potato
raisins
rice
shrimp
sugar
tomato
yogurt

Community

beach
hospital
park
supermarket
university

Grammar

Singular/Plural

It has one bedroom.
It has two bedrooms.

There's a nice refrigerator.
There are four windows.

That sofa? Put **it** in the living room.
Those chairs? Put **them** in the dining room.

Where are the   carrots?   /s/
             potato**es**?   /z/
             peach**es**?   /ɪz/

Count/Non-Count Nouns

Count

There aren't any more   cookie**s**.
                       tomato**es**.
                       apple**s**.

Where are the   carrot**s**?
             potato**es**?
             peach**es**?

These egg roll**s** are delicious!

Non-Count

There isn't any more   milk.
                    bread.
                    cheese.

Where's the   butter?
            sugar?
            rice?

This cake is delicious.

This/That/These/Those

Where do you want **this** sofa?
    That sofa?
How about **these** chairs?
    Those chairs?

There Is/There Are

Is there a refrigerator?
    Yes, **there is. There's** a refrigerator in the kitchen.

How many windows **are there?**
    There are four windows.

There isn't any more milk.
There aren't any more cookies.

Articles: A/An

A cookie.   **An** apple.
A tomato.   **An** egg.
A banana.   **An** orange.

Article: The

Where are **the** carrots?
Where's **the** butter?

Some/Any

I'll get **some** more.
There aren't **any** more cookies.

Imperatives

Put it in the living room.
Please put them in the dining room.

Have/Has

I **have** an apartment for you.
It **has** two bedrooms.

Simple Present Tense vs. To Be

How much **is** the rent?

Do you want to see the apartment?
Does that include utilities?

Cardinal Numbers: 100–999

100   one hundred
200   two hundred
300   three hundred
•   •
•   •
900   nine hundred
999   nine hundred (and) ninety-nine

Functions and Conversation Strategies in this chapter are listed in the Appendix, page A-2.

What Job Do You Have Open?
Can I Come In for an Interview?
I'm a Very Experienced Sales Clerk
I'm Sure I Can Learn Quickly
Are You Currently Employed?
Can You Tell Me a Little More About the Position?
Can You Tell Me About the Work Schedule
and the Salary?
Tell Me a Little More About Yourself

• Asking for and Reporting Information
• Asking for and Reporting Additional Information
• Ability/Inability • Certainty/Uncertainty
• Checking and Indicating Understanding • Hesitating

What Job Do You Have Open?

A. Can I talk to the manager?

B. Yes. I'm the manager.

A. I saw your "help wanted" sign. What job do you have open?

B. We're looking for a cook.

A. I'd like to apply.

B. Can you make eggs and sandwiches?

A. Yes, I can.

B. Okay. Here's an application form.

A. Thank you.

make eggs and sandwiches?

1. fix cars?

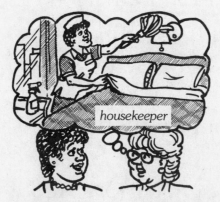

2. clean rooms and make beds?

3. use a cash register?

4. operate kitchen equipment?

5. lift heavy boxes?

"WHAT JOB DO YOU HAVE OPEN?"

Now present your own conversations.

Can I Come In for an Interview?

Ann Kramer

A. I'm calling about your ad for a secretary. Is that job still open?

B. Yes, it is. Can you type?

A. Yes, I can. Can I come in for an interview?

B. Yes. What's your name?

A. Ann Kramer.

B. Can you come in on Monday at 10:00?*

A. On Monday at 10:00? Yes. Thanks very much.

Peter Grant

1. Tuesday
2:00

Gary Johnson

2. Wednesday
3:00

Brenda Hall

3. Thursday
1:30†

Norman Taylor

4. Friday
9:30

Maria Lopez

5. Monday
11:30

Now present your own conversations.

* 10:00 = ten o'clock   † 1:30 = one thirty

I'm a Very Experienced Sales Clerk

A. I'm a very experienced sales clerk.

B. Tell me about your skills.

A. I know how to talk with customers and I can use a cash register.

B. I see. And do you know how to take inventory?

A. Yes, I do. I can take inventory very well.

1. secretary

2. medical technician

3. actor

4. custodian

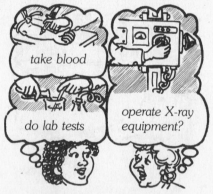

5. chef

Now present your own conversations.

I'm Sure I Can Learn Quickly

use a copying machine?

A. Can you use a copying machine?

B. No, I can't.   But I'm sure I can learn quickly.

A. Hmm.   We really need somebody who can use a copying machine.

B. I understand.   I know I can learn very quickly.

A. Are you sure?

B. Yes.   I'm positive.

make salads?

1.

operate a forklift?

2.

repair vacuum cleaners and toasters?

3.

use word-processing equipment?

4.

play rock 'n roll?

5.

"I'M SURE I CAN LEARN QUICKLY"

Now present your own conversations.

Are You Currently Employed?

yes
Tyler's Department Store
3 years

no
the Seven Seas Restaurant
1 year

A. Are you currently employed?

B. Yes, I am. I work at Tyler's Department Store.

A. And what is your position there?

B. I'm a salesperson.

A. How long have you worked there?

B. Three years.

A. Are you currently employed?

B. No, not at the moment. My last job was at the Seven Seas Restaurant.

A. And what was your position there?

B. I was a waiter.

A. How long did you work there?

B. One year.

1. yes
   the Crown Insurance
   Company
   2 years

2. no
   the Broadway Coffee
   Shop
   9 months

3. no
   the Adult Learning
   Center
   5 years

4. yes
   the Ajax Security
   Company
   7 months

5. no
   the Rinkydink Brothers
   Circus
   30 years

"ARE YOU CURRENTLY EMPLOYED?"

Now present your own conversations.

* ESL = English as a Second Language

Can You Tell Me a Little More About the Position?

a stock clerk

A. Can you tell me a little more about the position?

B. Certainly. What do you want to know?

A. What are the job responsibilities of a stock clerk here?

B. A stock clerk stocks the shelves and cleans the aisles. Do you think you can do that?

A. Yes, definitely! I stock the shelves and clean the aisles in my present job.

1. a housekeeper

2. a waiter

3. a salesperson

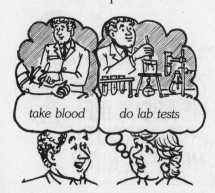

4. a medical technician

5. a security guard

Now present your own conversations.

* I.D. = identification

Can You Tell Me About the Work Schedule and the Salary?

9:00 – 5:30
1:00
five dollars ($5.00)
an hour

A. Can you tell me about the work schedule?

B. Yes.   Hours are from nine (9:00)* to five thirty (5:30), with a lunch break at one (1:00).*

A. I see.   And may I ask about the salary?

B. Yes.   The salary is five dollars ($5.00) an hour.   Do you have any other questions?

A. No.   I don't think so.

8:30 – 5:00
12:30
six dollars ($6.00) an hour

1.

8:00 – 4:30
12 noon
two hundred and fifty
dollars ($250) a week

2.

7:30 – 6:00
11:30
fifty dollars ($50) a day

3.

7:00 – 3:30
11:00
fifteen thousand dollars
($15,000) a year

4.

9:00 – 5:00
noon
eighteen thousand dollars
($18,000) a year

5.

"CAN YOU TELL ME ABOUT THE WORK SCHEDULE AND THE SALARY?"

Now present your own conversations.

* 9:00 = "nine o'clock" or "nine"
  1:00 = "one o'clock" or "one"

INTERCHANGE
Tell Me a Little More About Yourself

A. Before we finish, tell me a little more about yourself.

B. All right. Let's see . . . I'm married. My husband's name is Richard. He's a security guard at the National Motors factory. We have two children, a son and a daughter.

A. And where are you originally from?

B. I'm from Dallas.

A. Do you have any hobbies or special interests?

B. Yes. I play the piano and I take dance lessons.

A. I see. Tell me, do YOU have any questions for ME?

B. No, I don't think so. I appreciate the time you've taken to talk with me.

A. My pleasure. You'll hear from us soon.

B. Thank you very much.

A. Before we finish, tell me a little more about yourself.

B. All right. Let's see . . . _____.

A. And where are you originally from?

B. I'm from _____.

A. Do you have any hobbies or special interests?

B. Yes. I _____.

A. I see. Tell me, do YOU have any questions for ME?

B. No, I don't think so. I appreciate the time you've taken to talk with me.

A. My pleasure. You'll hear from us soon.

B. Thank you very much.

You're at a job interview. Create an original conversation using the model dialog above as a guide. Feel free to adapt and expand the model any way you wish.

Topic Vocabulary

Occupations

actor
cashier
chef
clown
cook
custodian
data processor
dishwasher
driver
ESL teacher
housekeeper
lab technician
manager
mechanic
medical technician
office assistant
sales clerk
salesperson
science teacher
secretary
security guard
stock clerk
typist
waiter
waitress

Job Skills

act
bake
check *I.D. cards*
clean *rooms*
clean *the aisles*
cook *American food*
dance
do *lab tests*
drive *a truck*
file
fix *cars*
guard *the building entrance*
help *customers*
lift *heavy boxes*
make *beds*
make *eggs and sandwiches*
make *salads*
operate *a forklift*
operate *a heating system*
operate *kitchen equipment*
operate *office equipment*
operate *X-ray equipment*
play *rock 'n roll*
prepare *international food*
repair *things*
repair *vacuum cleaners and toasters*
serve *the food*

sing
stock *the shelves*
take *blood*
take *inventory*
take *orders*
take *shorthand*
talk *with customers*
teach *Biology*
type
use *a cash register*
use *a computer*
use *a copying machine*
use *cleaning equipment*
use *laboratory equipment*
use *word-processing equipment*

Family Members

children
daughter
husband
son

Getting a Job

ad
application form
employed
experienced

"help wanted" sign
hobbies
hours
interview
job
job responsibilities
lunch break
position
salary
skills
special interests
work schedule

Days of the Week

Sunday
Monday
Tuesday
Wednesday
Thursday
Friday
Saturday

Time

hour
day
week
month
year

Grammar

Can

Can you make eggs and sandwiches?
  Yes, I **can.**
  No, I **can't.**

I **can** use a cash register.
We really need somebody who
  can use a copying machine.

Can I talk to the manager?
Can you tell me a little more
  about the position?

Simple Present Tense

/s/
      I   stock   the shelves.
A stock clerk   stock**s**   the shelves

/z/
      I   clean   rooms.
A housekeeper   clean**s**   rooms.

/ɪz/
      I   use   a cash register.
A salesperson   use**s**   a cash register.

Do you have any hobbies?

May

May I ask about the salary?

Time Expressions

1:00	one o'clock (one)
2:00	two o'clock (two)
3:00	three o'clock (three)
•	•
•	•
12:00	twelve o'clock (twelve)
1:30	one thirty
2:30	two thirty
3:30	three thirty
•	•
•	•
12:30	twelve thirty

On Monday **at** 10:00.

Hours are **from** 9:00 **to** 5:30.

The salary is $5.00   **an hour.**
                $250   **a week.**
                 $50   **a day.**
             $15,000   **a year.**

To Be

Are you currently employed?
  Yes, I **am.**
What **is** your position there?
  I'm a salesperson.

am / is / are

am   **I'm** married.
is   My husband's name **is**
        Richard.
        He's a security guard.
are   Where **are** you originally
        from?

Past Tense: Preview

My last job **was** at the Seven
  Seas Restaurant.

What **was** your position there?
  I **was** a waiter.

How long **did** you work there?
  One year.

Cardinal Numbers: 1,000–1,000,000

1,000	one thousand
2,000	two thousand
3,000	three thousand
•	•
•	•
10,000	ten thousand
100,000	one hundred thousand
1,000,000	one million

Functions and Conversation Strategies in this chapter are listed in the Appendix, page A-3.

• Imperatives • Have • Can • Should
• Simple Present Tense vs. To Be
• Present Continuous Tense • Short Answers
• Time Expressions • Possessive Nouns
• Prepositions of Location • Count/Non-Count Nouns

I Have a Headache
What Do You Recommend?
Do You Want to Make an Appointment?
Do You Smoke?
Touch Your Toes
You Should Go on a Diet
Take One Tablet Three Times a Day
I Want to Report an Emergency!

• Asking for and Reporting Information • Instructing
• Advice–Suggestions • Directions–Location
• Checking and Indicating Understanding
• Initiating a Topic

I Have a Headache

a headache

A. You know . . . you don't look very well.
Are you feeling okay?

B. No, not really.

A. What's the matter?

B. I have a headache.

A. I'm sorry to hear that.

an earache

1.

a stomachache

2.

a toothache

3.

a sore throat

4.

a backache

5.

"I HAVE A HEADACHE"

Now present your own conversations.

What Do You Recommend?

a bad cold — Maxi-Fed Cold Medicine

in Aisle 2 on the right

A. Excuse me. Can you help me?

B. Yes.

A. I have a bad cold. What do you recommend?

B. I recommend Maxi-Fed Cold Medicine.

A. Maxi-Fed Cold Medicine?

B. Yes.

A. Where can I find it?

B. It's in Aisle 2 on the right.

A. Thanks.

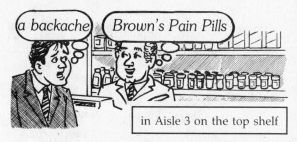

a backache — Brown's Pain Pills

in Aisle 3 on the top shelf

A. Excuse me. Can you help me?

B. Yes.

A. I have a backache. What do you recommend?

B. I recommend Brown's Pain Pills.

A. Brown's Pain Pills?

B. Yes.

A. Where can I find them?

B. They're in Aisle 3 on the top shelf.

A. Thank you.

a headache — Taylor's Aspirin

1. in Aisle 1 on the left

a stomachache — Tummy-Aid Tablets

2. in Aisle 4 on the bottom shelf

an earache — Drum's Ear Drops

3. in Aisle 2 on the middle shelf

a bad cough — Silence Cough Syrup

4. in the back near the aspirin

a terrible sore throat — Victor's Throat Lozenges

5. in the front near the cash register

"WHAT DO YOU RECOMMEND?"

Now present your own conversations.

Do You Want to Make an Appointment?

John Stevens isn't feeling very well.

A. Doctor's Office.

B. Hello. This is John Stevens. I'm not feeling very well.

A. What's the problem?

B. My right foot hurts very badly.

A. I see. Do you want to make an appointment?

B. Yes, please.

A. Can you come in tomorrow morning at 9:15?*

B. Tomorrow morning at 9:15? Yes. That's fine. Thank you.

1. Karen Fuller isn't feeling very well.

2. Sally Wilson's son isn't feeling very well.

3. Mr. Beck's daughter isn't feeling very well.

4. Ms. Wong isn't feeling very well.

5. Charlie Green's parrot, Willy, isn't feeling very well.

Now present your own conversations.

* 9:15 = nine fifteen
† 11:45 = eleven forty-five

52

Do You Smoke?

A. I have just one more question.

B. All right.

A. Do you smoke?

B. No, I don't.

A. Okay. I think that's all the information I need for your medical history. The doctor will see you shortly.

B. Thank you.

Are you allergic to penicillin?

No, . . .

1.

Do you drink?

No, . . .

2.

Is there a history of heart disease in your family?

No, . . .

3.

Do you have any allergies?

No, . . .

4.

Are you currently taking any medication?

No, . . .

5.

"DO YOU SMOKE?"

Now present your own conversations.

Touch Your Toes

A. Touch your toes.
B. My toes?
A. Yes.

A. Take off your shirt.
B. My shirt?
A. Yes.

A. Sit on the table.
B. On the table?
A. Yes.

A. Hold your breath.
B. Hold my breath?
A. Yes.

1.

2.

3.

4.

5.

Now present your own conversations.

You Should Go on a Diet

weight
go on a diet
lose 15 pounds

A. I'm concerned about your weight.

B. My weight?

A. Yes.   You should go on a diet.

B. I see.

A. I suggest that you lose 15 pounds.

B. I understand.   Thank you for the advice.

1. lungs
stop smoking
quit immediately

2. back
exercise daily
do sit-ups

3. blood pressure
change your diet
stop eating salty and
    fatty foods

4. gums
use dental floss
use it daily

5. life style
slow down
take a vacation

Now present your own
conversations.

Take One Tablet Three Times a Day

1 tablet 3 times a day

A. Here's your medicine.

B. Thank you.

A. Be sure to follow the directions on the label. Take one tablet three times a day.

B. I understand. One tablet three times a day.

A. That's right.

1 pill 4 times a day

1.

2 tablets before each meal

2.

1 teaspoon twice a day

3.

2 capsules after each meal

4.

1 teaspoon 3 times a day

5.

"TAKE ONE TABLET THREE TIMES A DAY"

Now present your own conversations.

INTERCHANGE
I Want to Report an Emergency!

A. Police.

B. I want to report an emergency!

A. Yes?

B. I think my father is having a heart attack!

A. What's your name?

B. Diane Perkins.

A. And the address?

B. 76 Lake Street.

A. Telephone number?

B. 293-7637.

A. All right. We'll be there right away.

B. Thank you.

Diane Perkins
76 Lake Street
293-7637

1. Neal Stockman
193 Davis Avenue
458-9313

2. Janet Brown
17 Park Road
963-2475

3. Carol Weaver
1440 Lexington Boulevard
354-6260

4. Henry Stewart
5 Linden Lane
723-0980

You're reporting an emergency. Create an original conversation using the model dialog above as a guide. Feel free to adapt and expand the model any way you wish.

Topic Vocabulary

Health

allergies
backache
bleeding
choking
cold
cough
dizzy
earache
headache
heart attack
heart disease
sore throat
stiff neck
stomachache
toothache

back
ear
foot
gums
lungs
neck
toes

blood pressure
diet
life style
weight

Personal Information

name
address
telephone number

Medicine

aspirin
cold medicine
cough syrup
ear drops
medication
pain pills
penicillin
throat lozenges

capsule
pill
tablet
teaspoon

Emergencies

ambulance
emergency
fire department
hospital
police
police emergency unit

Family Members

daughter
father
son
wife

Grammar

Imperatives

Touch your toes.
Be sure to follow the directions on the label.

Have

I **have** a headache.

Can

Can you help me?

Should

You **should** go on a diet.

Simple Present Tense vs. To Be

Do you smoke?
No, I **don't.**

Are you allergic to penicillin?
No, **I'm not.**
Is there a history of heart disease in your family?
No, there **isn't.**

Present Continuous Tense

I'm not **feeling** very well.
He's feeling very dizzy.
My ears **are** ring**ing.**

Short Answers

No, I don't.
No, I'm not.

No, there isn't.

Time Expressions

1:15	one fifteen
2:15	two fifteen
3:15	three fifteen
•	•
•	•
12:15	twelve fifteen
1:45	one forty-five
2:45	two forty-five
3:45	three forty-five
•	•
•	•
12:45	twelve forty-five

this morning
this afternoon
tomorrow morning
tomorrow afternoon
this Friday
next Monday

tomorrow morning **at** 9:15

Take one tablet three **times a day.**
                     twice a day.
            before each meal.
            after each meal.

Possessive Nouns

Doctor**'s** Office.
Sally Wilson**'s** son isn't feeling very well.

Prepositions of Location

It's **in** Aisle 2 **on** the right.
It's **in** Aisle 2 **near** the aspirin.

Count/Non-Count Nouns

Count

I recommend Brown's Pain Pill**s.**
Where can I find **them**?
They're in Aisle 3.

Non-Count

I recommend Maxi-Fed Cold Medicine.
Where can I find **it**?
It's in Aisle 2.

Functions and Conversation Strategies in this chapter are listed in the Appendix, **page A-3.**

SCENES & IMPROVISATIONS
Chapters 4, 5, 6

Who do you think these people are?
What do you think they're talking about?
Create conversations based on these scenes and act them out.

1.

2.

3.

4.

5.

6.

7.

8.

- **CLOTHING** · **DEPARTMENT STORE**
- **MONEY** · **POST OFFICE**

- **Singular/Plural** · **Prepositions of Location**
- **Adjectives** · **Too + Adjective**
- **Ordinal Numbers** · **Want to**
- **Question Formation**

I'm Looking for a Shirt
May I Help You?
It's Too Short
Excuse Me. Where Are the Rest Rooms?
I'd Like to Buy This Watch
I Want to Return This Fan
I Want to Buy Some Stamps, Please
I'd Like to Mail This Package

- Want–Desire · Directions–Location
- Satisfaction/Dissatisfaction
- Attracting Attention · Gratitude
- Checking and Indicating Understanding
- Hesitating

I'm Looking for a Shirt

A. Excuse me. Can you help me?

B. Certainly.

A. I'm looking for a shirt.

B. Shirts are in Aisle 3.

A. Thank you.

A. Excuse me. Can you help me?

B. Certainly.

A. I'm looking for a tie.

B. Ties are on that counter.

A. Thank you.

A. Excuse me. Can you help me?

B. Certainly.

A. I'm looking for a dress.

B. Dresses are over there.

A. Thank you.

A. Excuse me. Can you help me?

B. Certainly.

A. I'm looking for a pair of pants.

B. Pants are on that rack.

A. Thank you.

1.

2.

3.

4.

5.

Now present your own conversations.

May I Help You?

A. May I help you?

B. Yes, please. I'm looking for a belt.

A. What size do you want?

B. Size 36.

A. And what color?

B. Black.

A. Okay. Let's see . . . a size 36 black belt. Here you are.

B. Thank you very much.

1.

2.

3.

4.

5.

Now present your own conversations.

* 15½ = fifteen and a half

It's Too Short

jacket

A. How does the jacket fit?

B. It's too short.

A. Do you want to try on another one?

B. Yes, please.

A. Okay. Here. I think this jacket will fit better.

B. Thanks very much.

pants

A. How do the pants fit?

B. They're too long.

A. Do you want to try on another pair?

B. Yes, please.

A. Okay. Here. I think these pants will fit better.

B. Thanks very much.

1. skirt

2. sneakers

3. blouse

4. gloves

5. suit

"IT'S TOO SHORT"

Now present your own conversations.

Excuse Me. Where Are the Rest Rooms?

on the 4th floor

the rest rooms?

A. Excuse me. Where are the rest rooms?
B. They're on the fourth floor.
A. The fourth floor?
B. Yes.
A. Thanks.

in the back of the store

the elevator?

A. Excuse me. Where's the elevator?
B. It's in the back of the store.
A. The back of the store?
B. Yes.
A. Thanks.

on the 1st floor

refrigerators?

1.

near the elevator

the dressing room?

2.

on the 3rd floor

TVs and radios?

3.

on the 2nd floor

bedroom furniture?

4.

in the basement

the Customer Service Counter?

5.

"EXCUSE ME. WHERE ARE THE REST ROOMS?"

Now present your own conversations

I'd Like to Buy This Watch

A. I'd like to buy this watch.

B. Okay. That's twenty-six ninety-five ($26.95).

A. Excuse me, but I don't think that's the right price. I think this watch is on sale this week.

B. Oh. You're right. It's ten percent (10%) off. I'm sorry.

A. That's okay.

B. With the tax, that comes to twenty-five dollars and forty-seven cents ($25.47).

A. I'd like to buy these earrings.

B. Okay. That's twelve fifty ($12.50).

A. Excuse me, but I don't think that's the right price. I think these earrings are on sale this week.

B. Oh. You're right. They're half price. I apologize.

A. That's okay.

B. With the tax, that comes to six dollars and fifty-six cents ($6.56).

1. necklace

2. boots

3. camera

4. stockings

5. typewriter

Now present your own conversations.

I Want to Return This Fan

fan
noisy

A. I want to return this fan.

B. What's the matter with it?

A. It's too noisy.

B. Do you want to exchange it?

A. No. I'd like a refund, please.

B. Okay. Do you have the receipt?

A. Yes. Here you are.

jeans
short

A. I want to return these jeans.

B. What's the matter with them?

A. They're too short.

B. Do you want to exchange them?

A. No. I'd like a refund, please.

B. Okay. Do you have the receipt?

A. Yes. Here you are.

1. purse
small

2. pajamas
tight

3. coat
heavy

4. videogames
easy

5. textbook
difficult

Now present your own
conversations.

I Want to Buy Some Stamps, Please

A. I want to buy some stamps, please.

B. I'm sorry. You're at the wrong window. You can buy stamps at Window Number 2.

A. Window Number 2?

B. Yes.

A. Thank you.

1. mail a package

2. buy a money order

3. send a registered letter

4. buy an aerogramme

5. file a change of address form

Now present your own conversations.

INTERCHANGE
I'd Like to Mail This Package

A. I'd like to mail this package.

B. Where's it going?

A. To Detroit.

B. How do you want to send it?

A. First class, please.

B. Do you want to insure it?

A. Hmm. I don't know.

B. Well, is it valuable?

A. Yes, it is. It's a camera I'm sending to my brother. Please insure it for fifty dollars ($50).

B. All right. That's four dollars and thirty-seven cents ($4.37), please.

A. I'd like to mail this package.

B. Where's it going?

A. To _____.

B. How do you want to send it?

A. First class, please.

B. Do you want to insure it?

A. Hmm. I don't know.

B. Well, is it valuable?

A. Yes, it is. It's a _____ I'm sending to _____. Please insure it for _____ dollars.

B. All right. That's _____ dollars and _____ cents, please.

You're mailing a package at the post office. Create an original conversation using the model dialog above as a guide. Feel free to adapt and expand the model any way you wish.

Topic Vocabulary

Clothing

belt
blouse
coat
dress
hat
jacket
necklace
purse
raincoat
shirt
skirt
suit
sweater
tie
umbrella
watch

boots
earrings
gloves
jeans
pajamas
pants
shoes
sneakers
socks
stockings

Department Store

aisle
basement
counter
Customer Service Counter
dressing room
elevator
price
rack
receipt
refund
rest rooms
sale
table
tax

bedroom furniture
camera
fan
radio
refrigerator
textbook
TV
typewriter
videogame

Colors

black
blue
brown
gray
green
red
white
yellow

Describing

big
difficult
easy
heavy
large
long
noisy
short
small
tight

Post Office

aerogramme
change of address form
money order
package
registered letter
stamps

first class
insure
window

Grammar

Singular/Plural

/s/
I'm looking for **a shirt.**
Shirts are in Aisle 3.

/z/
I'm looking for **a tie.**
Ties are in Aisle 3.

/ɪz/
I'm looking for **a dress.**
Dresses are in Aisle 3.

I'm looking for **a pair of** pants.
a pair of shoes.

I'd like to buy **this** watch.
I'd like to buy **these** earring**s.**

How does the
jacket fit?
What's the matter
with **it**?
It's too long.
Do you want to
try on **another**
one?

How do the pants
fit?
What the matter
with **them**?
They're too long.
Do you want to
try on **another**
pair?

Where's the elevator?
Where **are** the rest room**s**?

Prepositions of Location

Shirts are **in** Aisle 3.
on that counter.
in the back of the
store.
in the front of the
store.
near the elevator.
over there.

Adjectives

A **size 36 black** belt.
A **medium green** sweater.
A **small brown** raincoat.

It's too **short.**

Too + Adjective

It's **too short.**
They're **too long.**

Ordinal Numbers

1st   first
2nd   second
3rd   third
4th   fourth

Want To

I **want to** return this fan.

Do you **want to** insure it?
How do you **want to** send it?

Question Formation

Is it valuable?
Where's it going?

Do you want to insure it?
How do you want to send it?

Functions and Conversation Strategies in this chapter are listed in the Appendix, page A-4.

..

• EMPLOYMENT/ON THE JOB

• Past Tense • Imperatives • Object Pronouns
• Time Expressions • Can • Could
• Adjectives • Prepositions of Location
• Singular/Plural

Excuse Me. Where's the Supply Room?
Please Take This Box to Mr. Miller on the 3rd Floor
Can You Show Me How to Turn On This Machine?
Could You Tell Me How to Transfer a Call?
Could You Possibly Show Me How?
Did I Wash the Glasses All Right?
Did I Type the Letters All Right?
You're Required to Wear Your Helmet at All Times
I'm Free Now. What Do You Want Me to Do?

• Requests • Instructing • Attracting Attention
• Approval/Disapproval • Apologizing
• Checking and Indicating Understanding
• Asking for Repetition • Hesitating
• Focusing Attention

Excuse Me. Where's the Supply Room?

Bill   Patty

the supply room   down the hall   yesterday   company

A. Excuse me. Where's the supply room?

B. It's down the hall.

A. Thank you.

B. Are you a new employee?

A. Yes. I started yesterday. My name is Bill.

B. I'm Patty. Welcome to the company.

A. Thanks.

in the basement

the cafeteria   Julia   Dave

1. today
   office

in the employee lounge

the soda machine   Betty   Elaine

2. on Monday
   company

down the hall on the left

PERSONNEL

the Personnel Office   Carl   Gloria

3. yesterday
   store

the first door on the right

the bathroom   Edward   Ron

4. this morning
   restaurant

in the supply room

the first-aid kit   Hank   Sue

5. last week
   factory

"EXCUSE ME. WHERE'S THE SUPPLY ROOM?"

Now present your own conversations.

72

Please Take This Box to Mr. Miller on the 3rd Floor

A. Please take this box to Mr. Miller on the 3rd floor.

B. To Mr. Miller?

A. Yes.

B. I'm sorry, but I'm new here. What does he look like?

A. He's tall, with brown hair.

B. Okay. I'll do it right away.

> Please take this box **to Mr. Miller** on the 3rd floor.

He's tall, with brown hair.

height	weight	hair	
very tall	very thin	curly	brown
tall	thin	straight	black
average height	heavy		blond/blonde
short	very heavy	dark	red
very short		light	gray

> Please give this letter **to Mrs. Hill** in the Personnel Office.

1. She's short, with blonde hair.

> Please take this package **to Mr. Newton** in Shipping.

2. He's very tall and thin.

> Please get some clean glasses **from Fred** in the kitchen.

3. He's heavy, with curly dark hair.

> Please give these keys **to Ms. Johnson** at the front desk.

4. She's average height, with gray hair.

> Please get some typing paper **from Miss Walters** in Word Processing.

5. She's tall and thin, with straight black hair.

"PLEASE TAKE THIS BOX TO MR. MILLER ON THE 3RD FLOOR"

Now present your own conversations.

Can You Show Me How to Turn On This Machine?

Press this button.

turn on this machine

A. Excuse me. Can you help me for a minute?

B. Sure. What is it?

A. Can you show me how to turn on this machine?

B. Yes. Press this button.

A. I see. Thanks very much.

B. You're welcome.

Pull this chain.

1. turn off this light

Push this button.

2. open this door

Flip this switch.

3. start this dishwasher

Put in your time card like this.

4. punch in

Pull the lever like this.

5. stop the conveyor belt

"CAN YOU SHOW ME HOW TO TURN ON THIS MACHINE?"

Now present your own conversations.

Could You Tell Me How to Transfer a Call?

A. Excuse me. Could you help me for a minute?

B. Certainly. What is it?

A. Could you tell me how to transfer a call?

B. Sure. Press the red button. Then, dial the other office and hang up.

A. I see. First, I press the red button. Then, I dial the other office and hang up. Right?

B. Yes. That's right.

A. Thank you.

B. You're welcome.

Press the red button.

Dial the other office and hang up.

transfer a call

Set the amount.

Put the envelope in.

1. use the postage machine

Put a match in the hole at the bottom.

Turn on the gas.

2. light this oven

Pull the handle to close the door.

Push the black button.

3. operate the freight elevator

Put your name and employee number at the top.

List your hours and sign at the bottom.

Name: Ann Wade
#: 923002563
M 9-5
T 9-5
W 9-1
TH 9-7
F 9-5
Signed: Ann Wade

4. fill out this timesheet

Flip the switch to turn it on.

Hold the dish here and lift the handle.

5. use the ice cream machine

"COULD YOU TELL ME HOW TO TRANSFER A CALL?"

Now present your own conversations.

Could You Possibly Show Me How?

Take out your tray.

Close the drawer.

Turn the key on the side.

lock the cash register

A. How's your first day on the job going?

B. Fine.

A. Tell me, do you know how to lock the cash register?

B. No, I don't.   Could you possibly show me how?

A. All right.   First, take out your tray.   Then, close the drawer.

B. I'm sorry.   Could you please repeat that?

A. Sure.   First, take out your tray.

B. Um-hḿm.

A. Then, close the drawer.   Okay so far?

B. Yes.   I'm following you.

A. Then, turn the key on the side.   Have you got that?

B. Yes.   I understand.

A. Be sure to ask if you have any questions.

B. Okay.   Thank you very much.

A. How's your first day on the job going?

B. Fine.

A. Tell me, do you know how to _____?

B. No, I don't.   Could you possibly show me how?

A. All right.   First, _____.
   Then, _____.

B. I'm sorry.   Could you please repeat that?

A. Sure.   First, _____.

B. Um-hḿm.

A. Then, _____.   Okay so far?

B. Yes.   I'm following you.

A. Then, _____.   Have you got that?

B. Yes.   I understand.

A. Be sure to ask if you have any questions.

B. Okay.   Thank you very much.

Place the original on the glass.

Put down the cover.

Press the start button.

1. use the copying machine

Spray the wax on the floor.

Flip this switch to turn on the machine.

Go back and forth like this.

2. use the floor polishing machine

Write the date and the amount on the slip.

Place the slip and the credit card in the machine.

Ask the customer to sign and give the customer the top copy.

3. do a credit card sale

"COULD YOU POSSIBLY SHOW ME HOW?"

Now present your own conversations.

Did I Wash the Glasses All Right?

wash the glasses?

wash–washed

A. Did I wash the glasses all right?
B. Yes, you did. You washed them very well.
A. Thanks. I just wanted to check.

clean the supply room?

clean–cleaned

A. Did I clean the supply room all right?
B. Yes, you did. You cleaned it very well.
A. Thanks. I just wanted to check.

paint the ceiling?

paint–painted

A. Did I paint the ceiling all right?
B. Yes, you did. You painted it very well.
A. Thanks. I just wanted to check.

make the beds?

make–made

A. Did I make the beds all right?
B. Yes, you did. You made them very well.
A. Thanks. I just wanted to check.

stock the shelves?

1. stock–stocked

play that song?

2. play–played

operate the forklift?

3. operate–operated

write the reports?

4. write–wrote

give the speech?

5. give–gave

"DID I WASH THE GLASSES ALL RIGHT?"

Now present your own conversations.

Did I Type the Letters All Right?

type the letters?

You made several spelling mistakes.

type–typed

A. Did I type the letters all right?

B. Actually, you didn't. You typed them rather poorly.

A. Oh? What did I do wrong?

B. You made several spelling mistakes.

A. Oh. I'm sorry.

B. Don't worry about it. You're new on the job.

cook the eggs?

You used too much butter.

1. cook–cooked

inspect the car?

You didn't open the trunk.

2. inspect–inspected

set the table?

You put the napkins on the wrong side of the plates.

3. set–set

repair this TV?

You didn't fix the antenna.

4. repair–repaired

do that customer's hair?

You cut it too short.

5. do–did

"DID I TYPE THE LETTERS ALL RIGHT?"

Now present your own conversations.

You're Required to Wear Your Helmet at All Times

A. Johnson?

B. Yes, sir?*

A. Where's your helmet?

B. My helmet? Uh . . . I'm afraid I left† it in my car.

A. You know, you're required to wear your helmet at all times.

B. I'm sorry. I forgot.†

1. Karen

2. Peggy

3. Mr. Fuller

4. Miss Horner

Donald

5.

"YOU'RE REQUIRED TO WEAR YOUR HELMET AT ALL TIMES"

Now present your own conversations.

* sir (to a man)   † leave–left
  ma'am (to a woman)   forget–forgot

INTERCHANGE
I'm Free Now. What Do You Want Me to Do?

A. I'm free now.   What do you want me to do?

B. Please clean the kitchen shelves.

A. I did that already.

B. You did?

A. Yes.   I cleaned them an hour ago.

B. Oh, good.   Then please sweep the floor.

A. I did THAT already, too.

B. Really?

A. Yes.   I swept* it a little while ago.   Is there anything else I can do?

B. Hmm.   I can't think of anything at the moment.

A. Do you want me to set the tables for tomorrow?

B. Yes.   That's a good idea.   You know, you're an excellent new employee.

A. Thank you for saying so.   I'm very happy to be here.

A. I'm free now. What do you want me to do?
B. Please _____.
A. I did that already.
B. You did?
A. Yes.   I _____ an hour ago.
B. Oh, good.   Then please _____.
A. I did THAT already, too.
B. Really?
A. Yes.   I _____ a little while ago.   Is there anything else I can do?
B. Hmm.   I can't think of anything at the moment.
A. Do you want me to _____?
B. Yes.   That's a good idea.   You know, you're an excellent new employee.
A. Thank you for saying so.   I'm very happy to be here.

You're on the job and you're free at the moment.   Create an original conversation using the model dialog above as a guide.   Feel free to adapt and expand the model any way you wish.

* sweep–swept

CHAPTER 8 SUMMARY

Topic Vocabulary

Places of Work

company
factory
office
restaurant
store

Places on the Job

basement
bathroom
cafeteria
employee lounge
hall
Personnel Office
Shipping
supply room
Word Processing

Protective Clothing

gloves
hairnet
helmet
lab coat
safety glasses
uniform

Job Procedures

clean *the supply room*
close *the drawer*
cook *the eggs*
dial *the other office*
fill out *this timesheet*
fix *the antenna*
flip *this switch*
hang up
hold *the dish*
inspect *the car*
lift *the handle*
light *this oven*
list *your hours*
lock *the cash register*
make *the beds*
open *this door*
operate *the freight elevator*
paint *the ceiling*
place *the original on the glass*
press *this button*
pull *this chain*
punch in
push *this button*
put *a match in the hole*
put down *the cover*
put in *your time card*
repair *the TV*
set *the amount*

sign *at the bottom*
spray *the wax*
start *this dishwasher*
stock *the shelves*
stop *the conveyor belt*
sweep *the floor*
take out *your tray*
transfer *a call*
turn *the key*
turn off *this light*
turn on *the gas*
type *the letters*
use *the postage machine*
wash *the glasses*
write *the date*

Objects on the Job

cash register
conveyor belt
copying machine
first-aid kit
floor
forklift
freight elevator
key
lever
locker
machine
postage machine

soda machine
time card
timesheet
typing paper

Describing People

height
  very tall
  tall
  average height
  short
  very short

weight
  very thin
  thin
  heavy
  very heavy

hair
  curly
  straight
  light
  dark
  black
  blond/blonde
  brown
  gray
  red

Grammar

Past Tense

/t/
You wash**ed** them very well.

/d/
You clean**ed** it very well.

/ɪd/
You paint**ed** it very well.

Did I wash the glasses all right?
  Yes, you **did**.
  You **didn't**.

What **did** I do wrong?

make–made
Did I **make** the beds all right?
  You **made** them very well.

write–wrote
Did I **write** the reports all right?
  You **wrote** them very well.

give–gave
Did I **give** the speech all right?
  You **gave** it very well.

set–set
Did I **set** the table all right?
  You **set** it rather poorly.

do–did
Did I **do** that customer's hair all right?
  You **did** it rather poorly.

leave–left
I **left** it in my car.

forget–forgot
I **forgot**.

sweep–swept
Please **sweep** the floor.
  I **swept** it a little while ago.

Imperatives

Please take this box to Mr. Miller.

Press this button.

Time Expressions

I started **yesterday.**
       today.
       on Monday.
       this morning.
       last week.

Object Pronouns

You cleaned **it** very well.
You washed **them** very well.

Can

Can you help me for a minute?

Could

Could you help me for a minute?

Adjectives

He's **tall,** with **brown** hair.
He's **heavy,** with **curly dark** hair.

Prepositions of Location

It's **down** the hall.
It's **in** the basement.
It's **on** the left.

Singular/Plural

Where's your helmet?
Where **are** your gloves?

Functions and Conversation Strategies in this chapter are listed in the Appendix, **page A-5.**

9

- **RECREATION**
- **SOCIAL COMMUNICATION**
- **EMPLOYMENT/ON THE JOB** • **WEATHER**

- **Past Tense** • **WH-Questions** • **Future: Going to**
- **Want to** • **Like to** • **Like to vs. Like**
- **Can** • **Have to** • **Time Expressions**

What Do You Want to Do Today?
Let's Do Something Outdoors Today
Do You Want to Get Together Tomorrow?
I'm Afraid I Can't. I Have to Work Late
What Are You Going to Do This Weekend?
How Was Your Weekend?
What Movie Did You See?
What Do You Like to Do in Your Free Time?
Do You Like to Go to Movies?

- Want–Desire • Asking for and Reporting Information
- Invitations • Likes/Dislikes • Intention
- Obligation • Checking and Indicating Understanding

What Do You Want to Do Today?

see a movie

It's raining.

A. What do you want to do today?

B. I don't know. What's the weather like?

A. It's raining. Do you want to see a movie?

B. Sure. That's a good idea.

go skiing

1. It's snowing.

go swimming

4. It's hot.

have a picnic

2. It's sunny.

stay home and watch TV

5. It's cold.

go to a museum

3. It's cloudy.

"WHAT DO YOU WANT TO DO TODAY?"

Now present your own conversations.

Let's Do Something Outdoors Today

play tennis

go jogging

play–played

A. Let's do something outdoors today.

B. All right. But I don't want to play tennis. We played tennis last weekend.

A. Okay. What do you want to do?

B. I want to go jogging.

A. All right. That sounds like fun.

go swimming

play basketball

1. go–went

have a picnic

go to the beach

2. have–had

play golf

take a walk in the park

3. play–played

go sailing

go to the zoo

4. go–went

drive to the mountains

go skating

5. drive–drove

"LET'S DO SOMETHING OUTDOORS TODAY"

Now present your own conversations.

Do You Want to Get Together Tomorrow?

be hot
I heard it on the radio.

A. Do you want to get together tomorrow?

B. Sure.   What do you want to do?

A. I don't know.   What's the weather forecast?

B. It's going to be hot.

A. It is?

B. Yes.   I heard it on the radio.

A. Let's go to the beach.

B. Okay.   That sounds like fun.

1. be sunny
I read it in the paper.

2. rain
I saw the forecast on TV.

3. be cold
I heard it on the radio.

4. snow
I heard it on the
7 o'clock news.

5. be cloudy
I called the Weather
Information number.

Now present your own
conversations.

I'm Afraid I Can't. I Have to Work Late

go out for dinner **tonight**?

work late

A. Do you want to go out for dinner tonight?

B. Tonight? I'm afraid I can't. I have to work late.

A. That's too bad.

B. Maybe we can go out for dinner some other time.

go skiing **tomorrow**?

go to the dentist

1.

go dancing **tomorrow night**?

baby-sit

2.

see a play **this Saturday night**?

study

3.

go to a concert **this Sunday afternoon**?

visit my aunt and uncle

4.

go for a bike ride **this weekend**?

clean the yard

5.

"I'M AFRAID I CAN'T. I HAVE TO WORK LATE"

Now present your own conversations.

What Are You Going to Do This Weekend?

A. What are you going to do this weekend?

B. I'm going to paint my apartment. How about you?

A. I'm going to work in my garden.

B. Well, have a good weekend!

A. You, too.

1.

2.

3.

4.

5.

Now present your own conversations.

How Was Your Weekend?

A. Tell me, how was your weekend?

B. It was very nice.

A. What did you do?

B. I went skiing.   And how was YOUR weekend?

A. It was okay.

B. Did you do anything special?

A. Not really.   I stayed home and watched TV.

write letters | visit my son and his wife

1.

study | have a party

2.

read* | go to the beach

3.

clean my apartment | take* my daughter to a ballgame

4.

work on my taxes | drive to the mountains

5.

"HOW WAS YOUR WEEKEND?"

Now present your own conversations.

* read–read
   take–took

89

What Movie Did You See?

What movie did you see?

"Dancing in the Park"

at the movies

A. I called you yesterday evening, but you weren't home.

B. That's right. I wasn't. I was at the movies.

A. Oh. What movie did you see?

B. I saw "Dancing in the Park."

A. Did you enjoy it?

B. Yes. It was excellent.

Who did you hear?*

the Philadelphia Orchestra

1. at the concert hall

What play did you see?

"The Friendly Garden"

2. at the theater

What did you have?

moussaka

3. at the Greek restaurant

What game did you see?

the Yankees against the Red Sox

4. at the baseball stadium

Who did you go with?

Millie Hawkins

5. at the county fair

"WHAT MOVIE DID YOU SEE?"

Now present your own conversations.

* hear–heard

What Do You Like to Do in Your Free Time?

along the river   *run*   *in the park*   Where . . . ?

A. Tell me, what do you like to do in your free time?

B. I like to run.

A. Oh. That's interesting. Where do you like to run?

B. In the park. And how about you? Do YOU like to run?

A. Yes, but I don't like to run in the park. I like to run along the river.

B. Oh. That's interesting.

bake

bread   cakes and cookies

1. What . . .?

swim

at the "Y"*   at the lake

2. Where . . .?

knit

sweaters   baby clothes

3. What . . .?

read

novels   biographies

4. What kind of books . . .?

paint

people   trees

5. What . . .?

"WHAT DO YOU LIKE TO DO IN YOUR FREE TIME?"

Now present your own conversations.

* "Y" = YMCA or YWCA

INTERCHANGE
Do You Like to Go to Movies?

A. Tell me, do you like to go to movies?

B. Yes.   I like to go to movies a lot.

A. What kind of movies do you like?

B. I like comedies.   How about you?

A. I don't like comedies very much.   I like adventure movies.

B. Oh, I see.

A. Who's your favorite movie star?

B. Eddie Murphy.   How about you?

A. Harrison Ford.

A. Tell me, _____?

B. Yes. I like to/like _____ a lot.

A. _____ do you like?

B. I like _____. How about you?

A. I don't like _____ very much. I like _____.

B. Oh, I see.

A. Who's your favorite _____?

B. _____. How about you?

A. _____.

You're taking a break at work and you and a co-worker are "making small talk." In the exercises below, talk with your co-worker about music, TV, and sports, using the model dialog above as a guide. Feel free to adapt and expand the model any way you wish.

1. Do you like music?
   What kind of music* . . .?
   singer

2. Do you like to watch TV?
   Which program* . . .?
   TV star

3. Do you like [name of sport*]?
   Which team . . .?
   player

*	classical music rock music country music folk music jazz • • •

*	"Dallas" "Love Boat" "Wide World of Sports" • • •

*	baseball soccer football basketball hockey • • •

Topic Vocabulary

Weather

cloudy
cold
hot
rain
snow
sunny

Sports

baseball
basketball
football
golf
hockey
jogging
sailing
skating
skiing
soccer
swimming
tennis

Recreation and Entertainment

ballgame
baseball stadium
beach
bike ride
concert
concert hall
county fair
dancing
dinner
garden
lake
mountains
movie (the movies)
museum
park
party
picnic
play
restaurant
river
theater
TV
walk
zoo

Movies

adventure movies
comedies
dramas
mysteries
science fiction movies
westerns

Music

classical music
country music
folk music
jazz
rock music

Performers

actor
actress
movie star
player
singer
TV star

Family Members

aunt
children
daughter
grandchildren
grandfather
grandmother
son
uncle
wife

Grammar

Past Tense

How **was** your weekend?
   It **was** very nice.

I **wasn't** home.
You **weren't** home.

What **did** you do?
Did you do anything special?

We play**ed** tennis last weekend.

go–went
We **went** swimming.

have–had
We **had** a picnic.

drive–drove
We **drove** to the mountains.

read–read
I **read** a book.

take–took
I **took** my daughter to a ballgame.

see–saw
I **saw** "Dancing in the Park."

hear–heard
I **heard** the Philadelphia Orchestra.

WH-Questions

Who did you hear?
What movie did you see?
Where do you like to swim?
What kind of books do you like to read?
How was your weekend?
Which program do you like?

Future: Going To

It's **going to** be hot.

What are you **going to** do this weekend?
   I'm **going to** paint my apartment.

Want To

I **want to** go jogging.
I **don't want to** play tennis.

What do you **want to** do today?
Do you **want to** see a movie?

Like To

I **like to** run.
I **don't like to** run.

What do you **like to** do?
Do you **like to** run?

Like To vs. Like

Do you **like to** go to movies?
   I **like to** go to movies.

What kind of movies do you **like**?
I **like** comedies.
I **don't like** comedies.

Can

Maybe we **can** go out for dinner some other time.

I'm afraid I **can't**.

Have To

I **have to** work late.

Time Expressions

Do you want to go dancing
   tonight?
   tomorrow?
   tomorrow night?
   this Saturday **night**?
   this Sunday **afternoon**?
   this weekend?

Functions and Conversation Strategies in this chapter are listed in the Appendix, **page A-6.**

SCENES & IMPROVISATIONS
Chapters 7, 8, 9

Who do you think these people are?
What do you think they're talking about?
Create conversations based on these scenes and act them out.

1.

2.

3.

4.

5.

6.

7.

8.

CHAPTER-BY-CHAPTER SUMMARY OF FUNCTIONS AND CONVERSATION STRATEGIES

CHAPTER 1

Functions

Greeting People

Hello.
Hi. [less formal]

Nice to meet you.
　Nice meeting you, too.

How are you?
　Fine.
　Fine, thanks.

Introductions

Introducing Oneself

My name is *Carlos*.
I'm *Kim*.

Introducing Others

I'd like to introduce you to *my husband,
Michael*.

Asking for and Reporting Information

What's your name?
What's your last name?
And your first name?

Could you spell that, please?
　S-A-N-C-H-E-Z.

What's your address?
　10 Main Street.
And your telephone number?
　423-6978.

Where are you from?
　New York.
　I'm from *New York*.

Are you from *Tokyo*?

Are you *American*?

How about you?
And you?

CHAPTER 2

Functions

Asking for and Reporting Information

What city?
　Chicago.
What street?
　Hudson Avenue.

How do you spell that?
　N-I-E-L-S-O-N.

The number is *863-4227*.

Is this *328-7178*?

Is *Peter* there?
　No, *he* isn't. *He's at the supermarket*.

Where are you going?
　To *the library*.
　I'm going to *the library*.

And you?
How about you?

What are you doing?
　I'm *fixing my car*.

Greeting People

Hello.
Hi. [less formal]

Hello, *Fred*?
Hello. This is *Mike*.
Hello, *Steve*? This is *Jackie*.

How are you today?
How are you doing? [less formal]
　Fine.
　Fine, thanks.
　Pretty good.

Identifying

Hello. This is *Mike*.

Leave Taking

Nice seeing you.
　Nice seeing you, too.

I'll call back later.

Speak to you soon.

Good-bye.

Correcting

Giving Correction

No.
No, *it isn't*.

Apologizing

I'm sorry.
Sorry.

Gratitude

Expressing. . .

Thank you.

CHAPTER 3

Functions

Directions-Location

Asking for Directions

Can you tell me how to get to
＿＿＿＿＿?
Can you please tell me how to get to
＿＿＿＿＿?
Can you possibly tell me how to get to
＿＿＿＿＿?

Giving Directions

Walk THAT way.

Turn right.
Turn left.

Walk that way to *Second Avenue* and
　turn *right*.

Go *two* blocks to *Grove Street*.

Turn *left* on *Grove Street*.
Turn *right* at *Grand Avenue*.

Look for the *museum* on the *right*.

Take *the Second Avenue Bus* and get off
at *Park Street*.
Take *the West Side Expressway* and get
off at *Exit 14*.

Drive that way *two* miles.

Inquiring about Location

Is there a *post office* nearby?

Giving Location

There's a *post office* on *Main Street*.
It's on *Main Street*.
It's on *Main Street, next to the bank*.

It's $\begin{cases} \text{next to} \\ \text{across from} \\ \text{around the corner} \\ \text{from} \end{cases}$ the bank.

It's between *the library* and *the clinic*.

The *bus station* is $\begin{cases} \text{on the left.} \\ \text{on the right.} \end{cases}$

The *bus station* is on the *left, next to the
post office*.

Asking for and Reporting Information

Does this *bus* go to *Westville*?
It goes to *Riverside*.

Which *bus* goes to *Westville*?
The Number 30 bus.

Is this *Bus Number 42*?
Is this the *plane to Atlanta*?
Does this *bus* stop *at Center Street*?
Does this *plane* go to *Florida*?

Where do I *get off*?
At *Park Street*.

Attracting Attention

Excuse me.

Gratitude

Expressing . . .

Thank you.
Thank you very much.
Thanks.
Thanks very much.

Conversation Strategies

Checking and Indicating Understanding

Checking Another Person's Understanding

Okay so far?

Have you got that?

Checking One's Own Understanding

On Main Street?

I'm sorry. Did you say *the Second
Avenue bus?*

Indicating Understanding

Okay.

Uh-húh.

I see.

I understand.

I'm following you.

Asking for Repetition

I'm sorry. Could you please repeat
that?

WHERE *do I get off?*

CHAPTER 4

Functions

Asking for and Reporting Information

Can you describe it?

Is there *a refrigerator in the kitchen*?

How many *windows* are there?

There's *a very nice refrigerator in the
kitchen*.
There are *four windows in the living
room*.

How much is *the rent*?
It's *$700 a month*.
Does that include *utilities*?
It includes *everything except electricity*.

There isn't any more *milk*.
There aren't any more *cookies*.

What's in it?
What's in them?

Want-Desire

Inquiring about . . .

Do you want to *see the apartment*?

Where do you want *this sofa*?

Expressing . . .

We're looking for *a two-bedroom
apartment*.

Directions-Location

Inquiring about Location

Where's *the butter*?
Where are *the carrots*?

Giving Location

It's in *Aisle 3*.
They're in *Aisle J*.

Describing

It has *two bedrooms*.

Instructing

Put it *in the living room*.
Please put it *in the living room*.

Surprise-Disbelief

There isn't?
There aren't?

Attracting Attention

Excuse me.

Correcting

Giving Correction

No. "*J*."

Gratitude

Thank you.
Thanks.

Complimenting

Expressing Compliments

Mmm!

This *cake* is delicious!
These *egg rolls* are delicious!

It's excellent!
They're excellent!

Responding to Compliments

I'm glad you like it.
I'm glad you like them.

Thank you for saying so.

Conversation Strategies

Hesitating

Hmm.
Let me see.
Let me think . . .

Checking and Indicating Understanding

Checking One's Own Understanding

$700 *a month plus electricity?*

I'm sorry. Did you say "A?"

CHAPTER 5

Functions

Asking for and Reporting Information

What's your name?
   Ann Kramer.

Tell me about *your skills.*
Can you tell me about *the work schedule?*

What do you want to know?

What job do you have open?

Is that job still open?

Are you currently employed?
   Yes, I am. I work at *Tyler's Department Store.*
   No, not at the moment. My last job was at *the Seven Seas Restaurant.*

What is your position there?
   I'm a *salesperson.*
What was your position there?
   I was a *waiter.*

How long have you worked there?
How long did you work there?
   Three years.

What are the job responsibilities of a *stock clerk* here?
   A *stock clerk stocks the shelves.*

I *stock the shelves* in my present job.

Hours are *from nine to five thirty.*
The salary is *five dollars an hour.*

I'm *married.*

My *husband's* name is *Richard.*
He's *a security guard* at *the National Motors factory.*

We have *two* children, *a son and a daughter.*

Where are you originally from?
   I'm from *Dallas.*

Do you have any hobbies or special interests?
   I *play the piano.*

Asking for and Reporting Additional Information

Do you have any other questions?

Tell me a little more about *yourself.*
Can you tell me a little more about *the position?*

And may I ask *about the salary?*

Ability/Inability

Inquiring about . . .

Can you *make eggs and sandwiches?*
Can you *come in on Monday at 10:00?*

Do you know how to *take inventory?*

Do you think you can *do that?*

Expressing Ability

Yes.
Yes, I can.

I can *use a cash register.*
I can *take inventory* very well.

I know how to *talk with customers.*

Expressing Inability

No, I can't.

Certainty/Uncertainty

Inquiring about . . .

Are you sure?

Expressing Certainty

I'm sure *I can learn quickly.*
I know *I can learn very quickly.*

I'm positive.

Yes, definitely!

Requests

Direct, Polite

Can I *talk to the manager?*

Want-Desire

Expressing . . .

We're looking for *a cook.*

I'd like to *apply.*

Gratitude

Expressing . . .

Thank you.
Thank you very much.
Thanks very much.

Responding to . . .

My pleasure.

Appreciation

I appreciate *the time you've taken to talk with me.*

Conversation Strategies

Checking and Indicating Understanding

Checking One's Own Understanding

On Monday at 10:00?

Indicating Understanding

I understand.
I see.

Hesitating

Let's see . . .

CHAPTER 6

Functions

Asking for and Reporting Information

Are you feeling okay?
   No, not really.

What's the matter?
What's the problem?
I have *a headache*.
My *right foot* hurts very badly.
My *neck* is very *stiff*.
He's feeling very dizzy.
She has a bad *toothache*.
My *ears* are *ringing*.

My *father* is *having a heart attack*!
My *wife* can't *breathe*!
My *son* is *bleeding* very badly!
My *apartment* is on fire!
There's a *burglar in my house*!

Do you *smoke*?
Are you *allergic to penicillin*?
Is there a history of *heart disease* in
   your family?
Do you have *any allergies*?
Are you currently *taking any
   medication*?

I want to report an emergency!

What's your name?
   Diane Perkins.
And the address?
   76 Lake Street.
Telephone number?
   293-7637.

Instructing

Touch *your toes*.
Take off *your shirt*.
Sit *on the table*.
Hold *your breath*.
Lie *on your back*.
Look *at the ceiling*.
Say *"a-a-h"*!

Be sure to *follow the directions on the
   label*.

Take *one tablet three times* a day.
Take *two tablets* before *each meal*.
Take *two capsules* after *each meal*.

Advice-Suggestions

Asking for . . .

What do you recommend?

Offering . . .

I recommend *Maxi-Fed Cold Medicine*.

You should *go on a diet*.

I suggest that you *lose 15 pounds*.

Responding to . . .

Thank you for the advice.

Directions-Location

Inquiring about Location

Where can I find *it*?
Where can I find *them*?

Giving Location

It's in Aisle 2 {
on the right.
on the left.
on the top shelf.
on the middle shelf.
on the bottom shelf.
}
It's in the back near *the aspirin*.
It's in the front near the *cash register*.

Sympathizing

I'm sorry to hear that.

Attracting Attention

Excuse me.

Requests

Direct, Polite

Can you help me?

Gratitude

Expressing . . .

Thank you.
Thanks.

Identifying

Doctor's Office.
Police.
City Hospital.
Jones Ambulance Company.
Fire Department.
Police Emergency Unit.

Want-Desire

Inquiring about . . .

Do you want to *make an appointment*?

Ability/Inability

Inquiring about . . .

Can you *come in tomorrow morning*?

Asking for and Reporting Additional Information

I have just one more question.

Fear-Worry-Anxiety

I'm concerned about *your weight*.

Conversation Strategies

Checking and Indicating Understanding

Checking One's Own Understanding

Maxi-Fed Cold Medicine?
Tomorrow morning at 9:15?
My toes?
My weight?

One tablet three times a day.

Indicating Understanding

I see.
I understand.

Initiating a Topic

You know . . .

CHAPTER 7

Functions

Want-Desire

Inquiring about . . .

What *size* do you want?

Do you want to *try on another one*?

How do you want to *send it*?

Expressing . . .

I'm looking for *a shirt*.

I'd like to *buy this watch*.
I want to *return this fan*.
I want to *buy some stamps*, please.

I'd like *a refund*, please.

Directions-Location

Inquiring about Location

Where are *the rest rooms*?

Giving Location

Shirts are
{
in Aisle 3.
over there.
on that *counter*.
in the back of *the store*.
in the front of *the store*.
on the *fourth* floor.
near *the elevator*.
in *the basement*.
}

Satisfaction/Dissatisfaction

Inquiring about . . .

How *does the jacket* fit?

Expressing Dissatisfaction

It's too *short*.
They're too *long*.

Attracting Attention

Excuse me.

Gratitude

Expressing . . .

Thank you.
Thank you very much.
Thanks.
Thanks very much.

Requests

Direct, Polite

Can you *help me*?

Please *insure it for fifty dollars*.

Responding to Requests

Certainly.
All right.

Offering to Help

Making an Offer

May I help you?

Responding to an Offer

Yes, please.

Asking for and Reporting Information

That's *twenty-six ninety-five*.
That comes to *twenty-six ninety-five*.

It's *ten percent* off.
They're *half price*.

What's the matter with *it*?

Where's it going?
  To *Detroit*.

Is it *valuable*?
  Yes, it is. It's a *camera*.

Correcting

Giving Correction

Excuse me, but I don't think *that's the right price*.

You're *at* the wrong *window*.

Responding to Correction

Oh. You're right.

Apologizing

I'm sorry.
I apologize.

Granting Forgiveness

That's okay.

Conversation Strategies

Checking and Indicating Understanding

Checking One's Own Understanding

Okay. Let's see . . . *a size 36 black belt*.

The fourth floor?
Window Number 2?

Hesitating

Hmm.

CHAPTER 8

Functions

Requests

Direct, Polite

Please *take this box to Mr. Miller*.

Can you *show me how to turn on this machine*?

Could you *tell me how to transfer a call*?

Direct, More Polite

Can you help me for a minute?
Could you help me for a minute?

Could you possibly show me how?

Responding to Requests

Yes.
Sure.
Certainly.
All right.

Instructing

Press *this button*.
Pull *this chain*.
Push *this button*.
Flip *this switch*.

Put in your time card like this.

First, *take out your tray*.
Then, *close the drawer*.

Attracting Attention

Excuse me.

Johnson?

Approval/Disapproval

Inquiring about . . .

Did I *wash the glasses* all right?

Expressing Approval

You *washed them* very well.

Expressing Disapproval

You *typed them* rather poorly.

Apologizing

I'm sorry.

I'm sorry, but *I'm new here*.

Directions-Location

Inquiring about Location

Where's *the supply room*?

Giving Location

It's down the hall.
It's down the hall on the *left*.
It's in the *basement*.
It's the *first* door on the *right*.

Gratitude

Expressing . . .

Thank you.
Thanks.
Thank you very much.
Thanks very much.

Responding to . . .

You're welcome.

Introductions

Introducing Oneself

My name is *Bill*.
I'm *Patty*.

Greeting People

Welcome to *the company*.

Asking for and Reporting Information

What does he look like?

How's *your first day on the job going*?
Fine.

Tell me, _____?

What did I do wrong?

Where's *your helmet*?

Describing

He's *tall*, with *brown* hair.

Ability/Inability

Inquiring about . . .

Do you know how to *lock the cash register*?

Expressing Inability

No, I don't.

Correcting

Giving Correction

Actually, *you didn't*.

You *made several spelling mistakes*.

Granting Forgiveness

Don't worry about it.

Denying/Admitting

Admitting

I'm afraid *I left it in my car*.

Remembering/Forgetting

Indicating . . .

I forgot.

Offering to Help

Making an Offer

I'm free now. What do you want me to do?

Is there anything else I can do?

Do you want me to *set the tables*?

Complimenting

Expressing Compliments

You're an excellent *employee*.

Responding to Compliments

Thank you for saying so.

Obligation

Expressing . . .

You're required to *wear your helmet at all times*.

Conversation Strategies

Checking and Indicating Understanding

Checking Another Person's Understanding

Okay so far?

Have you got that?

Checking One's Own Understanding

To Mr. Miller?

First, *I press the button*. Then, *I dial the office*. Right?

Indicating Understanding

I see.

Yes. That's right.

Um-hmm.

I'm following you.
I understand.

Asking for Repetition

I'm sorry. Could you please repeat that?

Hesitating

Uh . . .

Focusing Attention

You know, *you're required to wear your helmet*.

CHAPTER 9

Functions

Want-Desire

Inquiring about . . .

What do you want to do?
What do you want to do today?

Do you want to *see a movie*?

Expressing . . .

I want to *go jogging*.

I don't want to *play tennis*.

Asking for and Reporting Information

Tell me, _____?

What's the weather like?
It's *raining*.

What's the weather forecast?
It's going to *be hot*.

I heard in *on the radio*.
I heard it *on the 7 o'clock news*.
I read it *in the paper*.
I saw *the forecast on TV*.
I called *the Weather Information number*.

How was *your weekend?*
  It was *very nice.*
What did you do?
  I *went skiing.*

Did you *do anything special?*

I was at *the movies.*

What *movie* did you *see?*
Who did you *hear?*

Invitations

Extending . . .

Do you want to *get together tomorrow?*

Accepting . . .

Sure.

That sounds like fun.

Declining . . .

I'm afraid I can't.

Maybe we can *go out for dinner* some
  other time.

Likes/Dislikes

Inquiring about . . .

What do you like to do in your free
  time?

Do you like to *run?*

Where do you like to *run?*
What do you like to *bake?*
What kind of *books* do you like to *read?*
Which *program* do you like?

Who's your favorite *movie star?*

Expressing Likes

I like to *run.*
I like to *run* a lot.

I like *comedies.*

Expressing Dislikes

I don't like to *run.*

I don't like *comedies* very much.

Intention

Inquiring about . . .

What are you going to do *this weekend?*

Expressing . . .

I'm going to *paint my apartment.*

Obligation

Expressing . . .

I have to *work late.*

Advice-Suggestions

Offering . . .

Let's *do something outdoors today.*

Ability/Inability

Expressing Inability

I'm afraid I can't.

Disappointment

That's too bad.

Leave Taking

Have a good weekend!
  You, too.

Satisfaction/Dissatisfaction

Inquiring about . . .

Did you enjoy it?

Expressing Satisfaction

Yes. It was excellent.

Conversation Strategy

Checking and Indicating Understanding

Checking One's Own Understanding

Tonight?

TOPIC VOCABULARY GLOSSARY

The number after each word indicates the page where the word first appears.

(n) = noun
(v) = verb

Clothing

belt 63
blouse 62
boots 66
coat 62
dress 62
earrings 66
gloves 64
hat 62
jacket 64
jeans 67
necklace 66
pajamas 67
pants 62
purse 67
raincoat 63
shirt 62
shoes 62
skirt 64
sneakers 64
socks 63
stockings 66
suit 64
sweater 63
tie (n) 62
umbrella 62
watch (n) 66

Colors

black 63
blue 63
brown 63
gray 63
green 63
red 63
white 63
yellow 63

Community

airport 13
bank 12
beach 30
bus station 18
clinic 12
department store 22
drug store 18
fire station 19
gas station 19
grocery store 19
hospital 19
hotel 19
laundromat 12
library 12
mall 13
movies (movie theater) 13
museum 13
park (n) 12
parking lot 19
police station 19
post office 12
school 12
shopping mall 23

supermarket 12
theater 24
train station 23
university 30
zoo 13

Countries

China 6
Egypt 6
Italy 6
Japan 6
Mexico 6
The Soviet Union 6

Days of the Week 41

Sunday
Monday
Tuesday
Wednesday
Thursday
Friday
Saturday

Department Store

aisle 62
basement 65
bedroom furniture 65
camera 66
counter 62
Customer Service
   Counter 65
dressing room 65
elevator 65
fan 67
price 66
rack 62
radio 65
receipt 67
refrigerator 65
refund (n) 67
rest rooms 65
sale 66
tax (n) 66
textbook 67
TV 65
typewriter 66
videogame 67

Describing

big 64
difficult 67
easy 67
heavy 67
large 64
long 64
noisy 67
short 64
small 63
tight 64

Describing People

height 73
   very tall 73
   tall 73
   average height 73
   short 73
   very short 73
weight 73
   very thin 73
   thin 73
   heavy 73
   very heavy 73
hair 73
   black 73
   blond/blonde 73
   brown 73
   curly 73
   dark 73
   gray 73
   light 73
   red 73
   straight 73

Emergencies

ambulance 57
emergency 57
fire department 57
hospital 57
police 57
police emergency unit 57

Employment

Getting a Job

ad 41
application form 40
employed 44
experienced 42
"help wanted" sign 40
hobbies 47
hours 46
interview 41
job 40
job responsibilities 45
lunch break 46
position 44
salary 46
skills 42
special interests 47
work schedule 46

Job Procedures & Skills

act 42
bake 42
check *I.D. cards* 45
clean *rooms* 40
clean *the aisles* 45
clean *the supply room* 78
close *the drawer* 76
cook *American food* 42
dance 42
dial *the other office* 75

do *lab tests* 42
drive *a truck* 41
file 42
fill out *this timesheet* 75
fix *cars* 40
flip *this switch* 74
guard *the building
   entrance* 45
hang up 75
help *customers* 45
hold *the dish* 75
inspect *the car* 79
lift *heavy boxes* 40
lift *the handle* 75
light *this oven* 75
list *your hours* 75
lock *the cash register* 76
make *beds* 40
make *eggs and sandwiches* 40
make *salads* 43
make *the beds* 78
open *this door* 74
operate *a forklift* 43
operate *a heating system* 42
operate *kitchen equipment* 40
operate *office equipment* 41
operate *the freight elevator* 75
operate *X-ray equipment* 42
paint 78
place *the original on the
   glass* 77
play *rock 'n roll* 43
prepare *international food* 42
press *this button* 74
pull *this chain* 74
punch in 74
push *this button* 74
put *a match in the hole* 75
put down *the cover* 77
put in *your time card* 74
repair *things* 42
repair *the TV* 79
repair *vacuum cleaners and
   toasters* 43
serve *the food* 45
set *the amount* 75
sign *at the bottom* 75
sing 42
spray *the wax* 77
start *this dishwasher* 74
stock *the shelves* 45
stop *the conveyor belt* 74
sweep *the floor* 81
take *blood* 42
take *inventory* 42
take *orders* 45
take *shorthand* 42
take out *your tray* 76
talk *with customers* 42
teach *Biology* 41
transfer *a call* 75
turn *the key* 76
turn off *this light* 74
turn on *the gas* 75
type 41
type *the letters* 79
use *a cash register* 40
use *a computer* 41

IRREGULAR VERBS

be	was/were	lose	lost
bleed	bled	make	made
break	broke	mean	meant
buy	bought	meet	met
catch	caught	overhear	overheard
come	came	pay	paid
cut	cut	put	put
do	did	quit	quit
drive	drove	read	read
eat	ate	ride	rode
fall	fell	ring	rang
feed	fed	run	ran
feel	felt	say	said
find	found	see	saw
fit	fit	send	sent
forget	forgot	set	set
get	got	sit	sat
give	gave	speak	spoke
go	went	stand	stood
hang	hung	steal	stole
have	had	sweep	swept
hear	heard	swim	swam
hit	hit	take	took
hold	held	teach	taught
hurt	hurt	tell	told
keep	kept	think	thought
know	knew	throw	threw
lay	laid	understand	understood
leave	left	wear	wore
lend	lent	write	wrote
lie	lay		

INDEX OF FUNCTIONS AND CONVERSATION STRATEGIES

INDEX OF TOPICS

INDEX OF GRAMMATICAL STRUCTURES